Monster Knits
for Little Monsters

HILLSBORO PUBLIC LIBRARIES
Hillsboro, OR
Member of Washington County
COOPERATIVE LIBRARY SERVICES

Monster Knits
for Little Monsters

20 SUPER-CUTE ANIMAL-THEMED
HAT, MITTEN, AND BOOTIE SETS TO KNIT

Nuriya Khegay

St. Martin's Griffin
New York

HILLSBORO PUBLIC LIBRARIES
Hillsboro, OR
Member of Washington County
COOPERATIVE LIBRARY SERVICES

MONSTER KNITS FOR LITTLE MONSTERS

Copyright © 2013 Quantum Publishing Ltd
Photography copyright © 2013 by Alexandra Vainshtein
All rights reserved. Printed in China. For information,
address St. Martin's Press, 175 Fifth Avenue, New York,
N.Y. 10010.

www.stmartins.com

The written instructions, photographs, designs, patterns,
and projects in this volume are intended for personal
use of the reader and may be reproduced for that
purpose only.

Library of Congress Cataloging-in-Publication Data
Available Upon Request

ISBN 978-1-250-02983-6 *5247 1363 8/13*

First U.S. Edition: August 2013

10 9 8 7 6 5 4 3 2 1

This book is published and produced by
Quantum Books
6 Blundell Street
London N7 9BH

QUMMKLM

Publisher: Sarah Bloxham
Managing Editor: Samantha Warrington
Editor: Cath Senker
Assistant Editor: Jo Morley
Pattern Checker: Claire Crompton

Designer: Rosamund Saunders
Illustrator: Stephen Dew

Photographer: Alexandra Vainshtein
Models: Allen Khegay, Valeria Khegay, Veronica
Hakhovich, Olivia Judith Bokk and Samuel Fisher
**Project Coordinator and Translator for Nuriya
Khegay:** Dmitriy Khegay

Production Manager: Rohana Yusof

Printed in China by 1010 Printing International Ltd

contents

introduction

Welcome to all who have picked up this book! Here you will find a showcase of my favorite designs for children's knitted coverall hats.

As a young mother living in New York, I realized there was a great need for warm hats for small children to protect them from the freezing cold and bitter wind. Having been trained in handicrafts by my own mother, I set about designing winter hats for my young children. I wanted them to be cozy, comfortable, and practical. And I wanted to create cute designs that would be irresistible to children.

Most of my garments have a unique coverall design to keep your child's head, ears, and neck warm and toasty. The practical pullover design ensures that your little one won't tug off their hat while you're out and about. All the garments have matching mittens, and some have booties too. With a coverall hat, you don't need a scarf as well. But I have also included three patterns, *wise owl* (page 44), *furry fox* (page 86) and *playful penguin* (page 110), which are not coverall but have a fastener under the chin to secure the hat. These have gorgeous matching scarves.

I've divided the projects into chapters. *Cuddly critters* (page 8) includes some of my simpler, more straightforward patterns, such as *honey bear*, which is knitted in one color. In *feathered friends* (page 28) you'll find a variety of original, eye-catching bird designs and a range of patterns from beginner to advanced. *Huggable horrors* (page 50) includes a variety of monsters and aliens that are sure to thrill your little one. These are mostly advanced patterns that will test your skills but prove well worth the effort. *Adorable animals* (page 74) has some animal favorites, such as *darling panda* and *cute shark*, and includes *furry fox*, with its extraordinary fox-like scarf. These are intermediate and advanced patterns. Finally, in *festive friends* (page 96) you'll find a lovely range of beginner and intermediate patterns for the festive season.

Before you embark on one of my projects, check the *knitting basics* section (page 114), which lists all the tools, materials, and techniques you will need and lots of practical advice. All my patterns are made with Lion Brand Jiffy acrylic yarn, which feels soft to the skin as well as being easy to wash; I advise you to use this yarn if possible. Note that you'll need to be able to do some simple crochet and a little basic embroidery for many of the patterns. Several projects use my special technique for closing fins and ears (page 138) so you may like to practice this before you start.

I hope that you will enjoy making my Monster Knits as much as I do, and that the projects will spark your imagination and lead you to create your own unique designs for the little monster in your life!

Nuriya Khegay

cuddly
critters

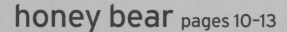

honey bear

This straightforward pattern makes a great starter project. The bee embroidery on the mittens forms an attractive detail, and cute booties complete the outfit.

COVERALL HAT,
MITTENS, AND BOOTIES
LEVEL: beginner
SIZES
6-12 months (12-24 months, 2-3 years)
Finished measurements
From "cheek to cheek" around the hat:
14 (14½, 15)in. (36 [37, 38]cm)
Mitten circumference: 5½ (6, 6½)in.
(1375 [15, 16.25]cm)
Mitten length: 5½ (6½, 7)in.
(14 [16.5, 18]cm)
Booties heel to toe:
3 (3 ⅜, 4½)in. (7.5 [9, 11]cm)
MATERIALS
HAT
Yarn:
1 x 3oz (85g) ball (135yd/123m) Lion
Brand Jiffy Yarn, 100% acrylic, Gold
Needles:
• 1 pair of US 3 (3.25mm) needles
• US 3 (3.25mm) circular needles
• Stitch marker
• Yarn needle
MITTENS
Main yarn:
Color A: 1 x 3oz (85g) ball (135yd/123m)
Lion Brand Jiffy Yarn, 100% acrylic, Gold
Small amounts:
Color B: Lion Brand Jiffy Yarn, 100%
acrylic, Black
Color C: Lion Brand Baby's First Yarn,
100% acrylic, Honey Bee
Needles:
• 4 x US 0 (2mm) double-pointed needles
• 4 x US 3 (3.25mm) double-pointed needles
• Yarn needle
BOOTIES
Yarn:
1 x 3oz (85g) ball (135yd/123m) Lion
Brand Jiffy Yarn, 100% acrylic, Gold
Needles:
• 4 x US 3 (3.25mm) double-pointed needles
• Yarn needle
GAUGE
16 sts and 25 rows = 4in./10cm square
in stockinette stitch worked with US 3
(3.25mm) needles.
19 sts and 28 rows = 4in./10cm square in k1,
p1 rib worked with US 3 (3.25mm) needles.

HAT

Using a pair of US 3 (3.25mm) needles, cast on 57 (61, 65) sts.
Rows 1-6 (6, 6): K1, p1 rib.
Rows 7- 30 (30, 32): Work in stockinette stitch, starting with a k row.
Row 31 (31, 33): K18 (19, 21), k2tog, k17 (19, 19), k2tog, turn. 55 (59, 63) sts.
Row 32 (32, 34): Sl, p17 (19, 19), p2tog, turn. 54 (58, 62) sts.
Row 33 (33, 35): Sl, k17 (19, 19), k2tog, turn. 53 (57, 61) sts.
Rep. rows 32 (32, 34) and 33 (33, 35) to row 54 (56, 62). 32 (34, 34) sts.
Row 55 (57, 63): Sl, *p1, k1* rep. from * to * 8 (9, 9) times, p1, k2tog, turn. 31 (33, 33) sts.
Row 56 (58, 64): Sl, *k1, p1* rep. from * to * 8 (9, 9) times, k1, p2tog, turn. 30 (32, 32) sts.
Rep. rows 55 (57, 63) and 56 (58, 64) to row 66 (68, 74). 20 (22, 22) sts.

It is easiest for beginners to work with a single color.

Neck ruff

Switch to US 3 (3.25mm) circular needles. Place a marker at the beginning of the round.

Round 67 (69, 75): Sl, *p1, k1* rep. from * to * 8 (9, 9) times, p1, k2tog, pick up 13 (12, 12) sts on one side of the hat, cast on 7 (7, 7) sts, join to work in the round, being careful not to twist, pick up 13 (12, 12) sts on the other side of the hat. 52 (52, 52) sts.

Rounds 68-77 (70-81, 76-89): K1, p1 rib.

Round 78 (82, 90): K2 (3, 3), yo, k2, yo, k11 (11, 11), yo, k2, yo, k11 (11, 11), yo, k2, yo, k11 (11, 11), yo, k2, yo, k9 (8, 8). 60 (60, 60) sts.

Round 79 (83, 91): K3 (4, 4), yo, k2, yo, k13 (13, 13), yo, k2, yo, k13 (13, 13), yo, k2, yo, k13 (13, 13), yo, k2, yo, k10 (9, 9). 68 (68, 68) sts.

Round 80 (84, 92): K4 (5, 5), yo, k2, yo, k15 (15, 15), yo, k2, yo, k15 (15, 15), yo, k2, yo, k15 (15, 15), yo, k2, yo, k11 (10, 10). 76 (76, 76) sts.

Round 81 (85, 93): K5 (6, 6), yo, k2, yo, k17 (17, 17), yo, k2, yo, k17 (17, 17), yo, k2, yo, k17 (17, 17), yo, k2, yo, k12 (11, 11). 84 (84, 84) sts.

Round 82 (86, 94): K6 (7, 7), yo, k2, yo, k19 (19, 19), yo, k2, yo, k19 (19, 19), yo, k2, yo, k19 (19, 19), yo, k2, yo, k13 (12, 12). 92 (92, 92) sts.

Round 83 (87, 95): K7 (8, 8), yo, k2, yo, k21 (21, 21), yo, k2, yo, k21 (21, 21), yo, k2, yo, k21 (21, 21),

yo, k2, yo, k14 (13, 13). 100 (100, 100) sts.

Round (88, 96) (two larger sizes only): K (9, 9), yo, k2, yo, k (23, 23), yo, k2, yo, k (23, 23), yo, k2, yo, k (23, 23), yo, k2, yo, k (14, 14). (108, 108) sts.

Round (89, 97) (two larger sizes only): K (10, 10), yo, k2, yo, k (25, 25), yo, k2, yo, k (25, 25), yo, k2, yo, k (25, 25), yo, k2, yo, k (15, 15). (116, 116) sts.

Round (98) (largest size only): K (11), yo, k2, yo, k (27), yo, k2, yo, k (27), yo, k2, yo, k (27), yo, k2, yo, k (16). (124) sts.

Round (99) (largest size only): K (12), yo, k2, yo, k (29), yo, k2, yo, k (29), yo, k2, yo, k (29), yo, k2, yo, k (17). (132) sts.

Rounds 84-89 (90-95, 100-105) (all sizes): K1, p1 rib.

Bind off. Weave in ends.

Ears (make 2)

Using a pair of US 3 (3.25mm) needles, cast on 25 sts, leaving an 8in./20cm tail for sewing the ears in place.

Rows 1-5: K1, p1 rib.

Cut tail long enough to weave in. Pull through all 25 stitches and remove them from needle. Pull the tail tightly and secure. Make a strong knot.

FINISHING

1 Sew the ears to the hat in the position shown using an invisible seam.

2 Weave in ends.

The back view of the hat, showing the neat fitting around the neck and shoulders.

Honey bear hat will keep little ears covered and it frames the face beautifully.

The little bees appear on the mittens, while the booties are in a classic easy-to-knit style.

MITTENS

(MAKE 2)

Cuff

Using US 0 (2mm) double-pointed needles and A, cast on 22 (24, 26) sts and divide evenly among 3 needles. Join to work in the round, being careful not to twist. Place a marker at the beginning of the round.
Rounds 1-10 (1-12, 1-14): Work in k1, p1 rib.

Thumb gusset

Switch to US 3 (3.25mm) double-pointed needles to work rest of mitten.
Round 1: M1R, knit to end of round. 23 (25, 27) sts.
Round 2: Knit.
Round 3: M1R, k1, M1L, knit to end of round. 25 (27, 29) sts.
Round 4: Knit.
Round 5: M1R, k3, M1L, knit to end of round. 27 (29, 31) sts.
Round 6: Knit.
Round 7: M1R, k5, M1L, knit to end of round. 29 (31, 33) sts.
Round 8: Knit.
Round (9, 9) (two larger sizes only): M1R, k7, M1L, knit to end of round. (33, 35) sts.
Round 9 (10, 10): K1, place 7 (9, 9) thumb stitches on waste yarn and rejoin to work hand stitches in the round, k21 (23, 25). 22 (24, 26) sts.

Hand

Rounds 10-22 (11-26, 11-28): Knit.
Closing up the top
Round 23 (27, 29): K2tog to end of round. 11 (12, 13) sts.
Round 24 (28, 30): Knit.
Round 25 (29, 31): K2tog to end of round. (If you get to the end of the round with only one stitch left, knit it.) 6 (6, 7) sts.
Cut a tail long enough to weave in. Pull it through all the stitches and remove them from the needles. Pull the tail tightly and secure. Weave in ends.

Thumb

Place 7 (9, 9) stitches from waste yarn onto US 3 (3.25mm) double-pointed needles. Rejoin yarn and pick up one extra stitch in the corner where mitten meets the gusset. 8 (10, 10) sts.
Rounds 1-6 (1-6, 1-8): Knit.
Round 7 (7, 9): K2tog to end of round. 4 (5, 5) sts.
Close up the top as for Hand.

FINISHING

With B and C (refer to photo), make a bee embroidery on both mittens:
1 Embroider the body of the bee with lazy daisy stitch. Bring up the needle from the center. Take it back down in the same place, leaving a loop of the size that you want. Bring the needle back up just inside the loop, at the other side. Cross over the loop and push the needle back down on the outside of the loop, to secure it.
2 Embroider the wings with satin stitch: work straight stitches (see page 137) close together across the shape.
3 Weave in ends.

BOOTIES

(MAKE 2)

Using US 3 (3.25mm) double-pointed needles, cast on 24 (26, 28) sts and divide evenly among 3 double-pointed needles. Join to work in the round, being careful not to twist. Place a marker at the beginning of the round.
Rounds 1-10 (1-12, 1-14): Work in k1, p1 rib.
Rounds 11-13 (13-15, 15-17): Knit.

Heel

Row 14 (16, 18): K12 (13, 14), turn.
Row 15 (17, 19): P12 (13, 14), turn.
Rep. rows 14 (16, 18) and 15 (17, 19) to row 19 (21, 23).
Row 20 (22, 24): K2, k2tog, k4 (5, 6), k2tog, turn. 22 (24, 26) sts.
Row 21 (23, 25): Sl, p4 (5, 6), p2tog, turn. 21 (23, 25) sts.
Row 22 (24, 26): Sl, k4 (5, 6), k2tog, turn. 20 (22, 24) sts.
Row 23 (25, 27): Sl, p4 (5, 6), p2tog, turn. 19 (21, 23) sts.
Work in rounds from now on.
Round 24 (26, 28): Sl, k4 (5, 6), k2tog, pick up 3 sts down side of heel, k12 (13, 14). 21 (23, 25) sts.
Round 25 (27, 29): Pick up 3 sts up side of heel, k21 (23, 25). 24 (26, 28) sts.
Rounds 26-40 (28-46, 30-52): Knit.
Closing up the toe
Round 41 (47, 53): K2tog to end of round. 12 (13, 14) sts.
Round 42 (48, 54): Knit.
Round 43 (49, 55): K2tog to end of round. (If you get to the end of the round with only one stitch left, knit it.) 6 (7, 7) sts.
Close up the top as for Hand.

fluffy bunny

This soft white hat with classic rabbit ears will delight any child. It uses basic crochet stitches for the pretty flowers decorating the hat and mittens.

COVERALL HAT AND MITTENS
LEVEL: beginner
SIZES
6-12 months (12-24 months, 2-3 years)
Finished measurements
From "cheek to cheek" around the hat:
14 (14½, 15)in. (36 [37, 38]cm)
Mitten circumference: 5½ (6, 6½)in.
(13.75 [15, 16.25]cm)
Mitten length: 5½ (6½, 7)in.
(14 [16.5, 18]cm)
MATERIALS
HAT
Main yarn:
Color A: 1 x 3oz (85g) ball (135yd/123m)
Lion Brand Jiffy Yarn, 100% acrylic, White
Small amounts:
Color B: Lion Brand Jiffy Yarn, 100%
acrylic, Light Pink
Color C: Lion Brand Jiffy Yarn, 100%
acrylic, Shocking Pink
Color D: Lion Brand Jiffy Yarn, 100%
acrylic, Apple Green
Color E: Lion Brand Baby's First Yarn,
100% acrylic, Honey Bee
Needles:
• 1 pair of US 3 (3.25mm) needles
• US 3 (3.25mm) circular needles
• 4 x US 3 (3.25mm) double-pointed
  needles
• Stitch marker
• US C-2 (2.75mm) crochet hook
• Yarn needle
MITTENS
Yarn:
Color A: 1 x 3oz (85g) ball (135yd/123m)
Lion Brand Jiffy Yarn, 100% acrylic, White
Color B: Lion Brand Jiffy Yarn, 100%
acrylic, Light Pink (a small amount)
Needles:
• 4 x US 0 (2mm) double-pointed needles
• 4 x US 3 (3.25mm) double-pointed
  needles
• Yarn needle
GAUGE
16 sts and 25 rows = 4in./10cm square
in stockinette stitch worked with US 3
(3.25mm) needles.
19 sts and 28 rows = 4in./10cm square
in k1, p1 rib worked with US 3 (3.25mm)
needles.

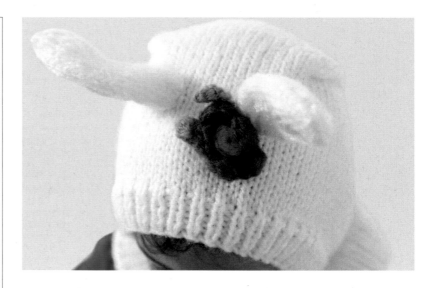

HAT

Using a pair of US 3 (3.25mm) needles and A, cast on 57 (61, 65) sts.
Rows 1-6 (6, 6): K1, p1 rib.
Rows 7- 30 (30, 32): Work in stockinette stitch, starting with a k row.
Row 31 (31, 33): K18 (19, 21), k2tog, k17 (19, 19), k2tog, turn. 55 (59, 63) sts.
Row 32 (32, 34): Sl, p17 (19, 19), p2tog, turn. 54 (58, 62) sts.
Row 33 (33, 35): Sl, k17 (19, 19), k2tog, turn. 53 (57, 61) sts.
Rep. rows 32 (32, 34) and 33 (33, 35) to row 54 (56, 62). 32 (34, 34) sts.
Row 55 (57, 63): Sl, *p1, k1* rep. from * to * 8 (9, 9) times, p1, k2tog, turn. 31 (33, 33) sts.
Row 56 (58, 64): Sl, *k1, p1* rep. from * to * 8 (9, 9) times, k1, p2tog, turn. 30 (32, 32) sts.
Rep. rows 55 (57, 63) and 56 (58, 64) to row 66 (68, 74). 20 (22, 22) sts.

Neck ruff

Switch to US 3 (3.25mm) circular needles. Place a marker at the beginning of the round.
Round 67 (69, 75): Sl, *p1, k1* rep. from * to * 8 (9, 9) times, p1, k2tog, pick up 13 (12, 12) sts on one side of the hat, cast on 7 (7, 7) sts, join to work in the round, being careful not to twist, pick up 13 (12, 12) sts on the other side of the hat. 52 (52, 52) sts.

The flower detail on the top can be knitted in different colors to suit little boys.

Rounds 68-77 (70-81, 76-89): K1, p1 rib. 52 (52, 52) sts. Join to work in the round, being careful not to twist.

Round 78 (82, 90): K2 (3, 3), *yo, k2, yo, k11* rep. from * to * 3 times, yo, k2, yo, k9 (8, 8). 60 (60, 60) sts.

Round 79 (83, 91): K3 (4, 4), *yo, k2, yo, k13* rep. from * to * 3 times, yo, k2, yo, k10 (9, 9). 68 (68, 68) sts.

Round 80 (84, 92): K4 (5, 5), yo, k2, yo, k15 (15, 15), yo, k2, yo, k15 (15, 15), yo, k2, yo, k15 (15, 15), yo, k2, yo, k11 (10, 10). 76 (76, 76) sts.

Round 81 (85, 93): K5 (6, 6), yo, k2, yo, k17 (17, 17), yo, k2, yo, k17 (17, 17), yo, k2, yo, k17 (17, 17), yo, k2, yo, k12 (11, 11). 84 (84, 84) sts.

Round 82 (86, 94): K6 (7, 7), yo, k2, yo, k19 (19, 19), yo, k2, yo, k19 (19, 19), yo, k2, yo, k19 (19, 19), yo, k2, yo, k13 (12, 12). 92 (92, 92) sts.

Round 83 (87, 95): K7 (8, 8), yo, k2, yo, k21 (21, 21), yo, k2, yo, k21 (21, 21), yo, k2, yo, k21 (21, 21), yo, k2, yo, k14 (13, 13). 100 (100, 100) sts.

Round (88, 96) (two larger sizes only): K (9, 9), yo, k2, yo, k (23, 23), yo, k2, yo, k (23, 23), yo, k2, yo, k (23, 23), yo, k2, yo, k (14, 14). (108, 108) sts.

Round (89, 97) (two larger sizes only): K (10, 10), yo, k2, yo, k (25, 25), yo, k2, yo, k (25, 25), yo, k2, yo, k (25, 25), yo, k2, yo, k (15, 15). (116, 116) sts.

Round (98) (largest size only): K (11), yo, k2, yo, k (27), yo, k2, yo, k (27), yo, k2, yo, k (27), yo, k2, yo, k (16). (124) sts.

Round (99) (largest size only): K (12), yo, k2, yo, k (29), yo, k2, yo, k (29), yo, k2, yo, k (29), yo, k2, yo, k (17). (132) sts.

Rounds 84-89 (90-95, 100-105) (all sizes): K1, p1 rib. Bind off. Weave in ends.

Ears (make 2)

Using US 3 (3.25mm) double-pointed needles and A, cast on 18 sts, leaving an 8in./20cm tail for sewing the ears in place. Join to work in the round, being careful not to twist. Place a marker at the beginning of the round.

Round 1-20: Knit.
Round 21: K2tog to end of round. 9 sts.
Round 22: Knit.
Round 23: Knit.
Round 24: K1, k2tog to end of round. 5 sts.
Cut a tail long enough to weave in. Pull through all 5 stitches and remove them from the needles. Pull the tail tightly and secure. Weave in ends.

Inner ear (make 2)

Using a pair of US 3 (3.25mm) needles and B, cast on 4 sts, leaving an 8in./20cm tail to sew the ears.

Rows 1-12: Garter st.
Row 13: K2tog 2 times. 2 sts.
Finish as for Ears.

FINISHING

1 Sew the inside of the ears onto the ears using an invisible seam. Weave in ends.
2 Fold the base of the ear in half and sew to the hat.
3 Weave in ends.

Flower (make 1 for hat and 2 for mittens)

Petals (make 3)

With C: Ch5. Join with sl st to form ring.
Round 1: 10sc through ring, sl st to top of first sc.
Round 2: Create a small petal in the first sc using the following pattern (sc, 3dc, sc). Continue creating a petal in alternate scs with the same pattern (5 petals total). Sl st to join with first sc of first petal. Fasten off.

Flower center (make 3)

With E, ch3. Join with sl st to form ring.
Round 1: 10sc through ring, sl st to top of first sc. Fasten off.

Leaves (make 6: 2 for hat and 4 for mittens)

With D, ch10, 1sl st in 2nd ch from hook, 1sc in 3rd ch from hook, 1sc in 4th ch from hook, 1hdc in 5th ch from hook, 1hdc in 6th ch from hook, 1dc in 7th ch from hook, 1dc in 8th ch from hook, ch2, sl st to first ch. Fasten off.

FINISHING

1 Sew the flower center to the leaves.
2 Sew the leaves to the flower.

The perky little ears stick up from the top of the hat.

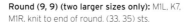

MITTENS

(MAKE 2)

Cuff

Using US 0 (2mm) double-pointed needles and B cast on 22 (24, 26) sts and divide evenly among 3 needles. Join to work in the round, being careful not to twist. Place a marker at the beginning of the round.

Rounds 1–10 (1–10, 1–10): Knit.
Switch to A.
Rounds 11–16 (11–16, 11–16): Work in k1, p1 rib.

Thumb gusset

Switch to US 3 (3.25mm) double-pointed needles to work rest of mitten.

Round 1: M1L, knit to end of round. 23 (25, 27) sts.
Round 2: Knit.
Round 3: M1L, K1, M1R, knit to end of round. 25 (27, 29) sts.
Round 4: Knit.
Round 5: M1L, K3, M1R, knit to end of round. 27 (29, 31) sts.
Round 6: Knit.
Round 7: M1L, K5, M1R, knit to end of round. 29 (31, 33) sts.
Round 8: Knit.

Round (9, 9) (two larger sizes only): M1L, K7, M1R, knit to end of round. (33, 35) sts.
Round 9 (10, 10): K1, place 7 (9, 9) thumb stitches on waste yarn and rejoin to work hand stitches in the round, k21 (23, 25). 22 (24, 26) sts.
Rounds 10–22 (11–26, 11–28): Knit.
Closing up the top
Round 23 (27, 29): K2tog to end of round. 11 (12, 13) sts.
Round 24 (28, 30): Knit.
Round 25 (29, 31): K2tog to end of round. (If you get to the end of the round with only one stitch left, knit it). 6 (6, 7) sts.
Finish as for hat Ears.

Thumb

Place 7 (9, 9) stitches from waste yarn onto US 3 (3.25mm) double-pointed needles. Rejoin and pick up one extra stitch in the corner where the mitten meets the gusset. Place a marker at the beginning of the round. 8 (10, 10) sts.
Rounds 1–6 (1–6, 1–8): Knit.
Round 7 (9, 9): K2tog to end of round. 4 (5, 5) sts.
Finish as for hat Ears.

FINISHING

1 Sew the flowers to the hat and mittens.
2 Weave in ends.

The flower decorations are repeated on the mittens. The mitten cuffs match the inner ears of the hat.

baby bear

This gorgeous baby-bear hat in a classic pale-brown shade has sweet little ears and a central cable detail on the hat and mittens.

COVERALL HAT AND MITTENS
LEVEL: intermediate
SIZES
6-12 months (12-24 months, 2-3 years)
Finished measurements
From "cheek to cheek" around the hat:
14 (14½, 15)in. (36 [37, 38]cm)
Mitten circumference: 5½ (6, 6½)in. (13.75 [15, 16.25]cm)
Mitten length: 5½ (6½, 7)in. (14 [16.5, 18]cm)
MATERIALS
HAT
Yarn:
1 x 3oz (85g) ball (135yd/123m)
Lion Brand Jiffy Yarn, 100% acrylic, Camel
Needles:
•1 pair of US 3 (3.25mm) needles
•US 3 (3.25mm) circular needle
•Cable needle
•Stitch marker
•Yarn needle
MITTENS
Yarn:
1 x 3oz (85g) ball (135yd/123m)
Lion Brand Jiffy Yarn, 100% acrylic, Camel
Needles:
•4 x US 0 (2mm) double-pointed needles
•4 x US 3 (3.25mm) double-pointed needles
•Cable needle
•Yarn needle
GAUGE
16 sts and 25 rows = 4in./10cm square in stockinette stitch worked with US 3 (3.25mm) needles.
19 sts and 28 rows = 4in./10cm square in k1, p1 rib worked with US 3 (3.25mm) needles.

HAT

Using a pair of US 3 (3.25mm) needles, cast on 58 (62, 66) sts.

Rows 1-6 (1-6, 1-8): Work in k2, p2 rib, starting with p2 (k2, p2).

Row 7 (7, 9): K24 (26, 28), p2, sl next 2 sts to cn and hold in front, k2, k2 from cn, k2, p2, k24 (26, 28). 58 (62, 66) sts.

Row 8 (8, 10): P24 (26, 28), k2, p6, k2, p24 (26, 28). 58 (62, 66) sts.

Row 9 (9, 11): K24 (26, 28), p2, k2, sl next 2 sts to cn and hold in back, k2, k2 from cn, p2, k24 (26, 28). 58 (62, 66) sts.

Row 10 (10, 12): P24 (26, 28), k2, p6, k2, p24 (26, 28). 58 (62, 66) sts.

Row 11 (11, 13): K24 (26, 28), p2, sl next 2 sts to cn and hold in front, k2, k2 from cn, k2, p2, k24 (26, 28). 58 (62, 66) sts.

Row 12 (12, 14): P24 (26, 28), k2, p6, k2, p24 (26, 28). 58 (62, 66) sts.

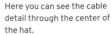

Here you can see the cable detail through the center of the hat.

Row 13 (13, 15): K24 (26, 28), p2, k2, sl next 2 sts to cn and hold in back, k2, k2 from cn, p2, k24 (26, 28). 58 (62, 66) sts.

Row 14 (14, 16): P24 (26, 28), k2, p6, k2, p24 (26, 28). 58 (62, 66) sts.

Row 15 (15, 17): K24 (26, 28), p2, sl next 2 sts to cn and hold in front, k2, k2 from cn, p2, p2, k24 (26, 28). 58 (62, 66) sts.

Row 16 (16, 18): P24 (26, 28), k2, p6,k2, p24 (26, 28). 58 (62, 66) sts.

Row 17 (17, 19): K24 (26, 28), p2, k2, sl next 2 sts to cn and hold in back, k2, k2 from cn, p2, k24 (26, 28). 58 (62, 66) sts.

Row 18 (18, 20): P24 (26, 28), k2, p6, k2, p24 (26, 28). 58 (62, 66) sts.

Row 19 (19, 21): K24 (26, 28), p2, sl next 2 sts to cn and hold in front, k2, k2 from cn, p2, p2, k24 (26, 28). 58 (62, 66) sts.

Row 20 (20, 22): P24 (26, 28), k2, p6, k2, p24 (26, 28). 58 (62, 66) sts.

Row 21 (21, 23): K24 (26, 28), p2, k2, sl next 2 sts to cn and hold in back, k2, k2 from cn, p2, k24 (26, 28). 58 (62, 66) sts.

Row 22 (22, 24): P24 (26, 28), k2, p6, k2, p24 (26, 28). 58 (62, 66) sts.

Row 23 (23, 25): K24 (26, 28), p2, sl next 2 sts to cn and hold in front, k2, k2 from cn, k2, p2, k24 (26, 28). 58 (62, 66) sts.

Row 24 (24, 26): P24 (26, 28), k2, p6, k2, p24 (26, 28). 58 (62, 66) sts.

Row 25 (25, 27): K24 (26, 28), p2, k2, sl next 2 sts to cn and hold in back, k2, k2 from cn, p2, k24 (26, 28). 58 (62, 66) sts.

Row 26 (26, 28): P24 (26, 28), k2, p6, k2, p24 (26, 28). 58 (62, 66) sts.

Row 27 (27, 29): K24 (26, 28), p2, sl next 2 sts to cn and hold in front, k2, k2 from cn, k2, p2, k24 (26, 28). 58 (62, 66) sts.

Row 28 (28, 30): P24 (26, 28), k2, p6, k2, p24 (26, 28). 58 (62, 66) sts.

Row 29 (29, 31): K24 (26, 28), p2, k2, sl next 2 sts to cn and hold in back, k2, k2 from cn, p2, k24 (26, 28). 58 (62, 66) sts.

Row 30 (30, 32): P24 (26, 28), k2, p6, k2, p24 (26, 28). 58 (62, 66) sts.

Row 31 (31, 33): K18 (19, 21), k2tog, k4 (5, 5), p2, sl next 2 sts to cn and hold in front, k2, k2 from cn, k2, p2, k4 (5, 5), k2tog, turn. 56 (60, 64) sts.

Row 32 (32, 34): Sl, p4 (5, 5), k2, p6, k2, p4 (5, 5), p2tog, turn. 55 (59, 63) sts.

Quite similar to honey bear, baby bear is a good project to try after you have mastered the beginner techniques.

Row 33 (33, 35): Sl, k4 (5, 5), p2, k2, sl next 2 sts to cn and hold in back, k2, k2 from cn, p2, k4 (5, 5), k2tog, turn. 54 (58, 62) sts.
Row 34 (34, 36): Sl, p4 (5, 5), k2, p6, k2, p4 (5, 5), p2tog, turn. 53 (57, 61) sts.
Row 35 (35, 37): Sl, k4 (5, 5), p2, sl next 2 sts to cn and hold in front, k2, k2 from cn, k2, p2, k4 (5, 5), k2tog, turn. 52 (56, 60) sts.
Row 36 (36, 38): Sl, p4 (5, 5), k2, p6, k2, p4 (5, 5), p2tog, turn. 51 (55, 59) sts.
Row 37 (37, 39): Sl, k4 (5, 5), p2, k2, sl next 2 sts to cn and hold in back, k2, k2 from cn, p2, k4 (5, 5), k2tog, turn. 50 (54, 58) sts.
Row 38 (38, 40): Sl, p4 (5, 5), k2, p6, k2, p4 (5, 5), p2tog, turn. 49 (53, 57) sts.
Row 39 (39, 41): Sl, k4 (5, 5), p2, sl next 2 sts to cn and hold in front, k2, k2 from cn, p2, k4 (5, 5), k2tog, turn. 48 (52, 56) sts.
Row 40 (40, 42): Sl, p4 (5, 5), k2, p6, k2, p4 (5, 5), p2tog, turn. 47 (51, 55) sts.
Row 41 (41, 43): Sl, k4 (5, 5), p2, k2, sl next 2 sts to cn and hold in back, k2, k2 from cn, p2, k4 (5, 5), k2tog, turn. 46 (50, 54) sts.
Row 42 (42, 44): Sl, p4 (5, 5), k2, p6, k2, p4 (5, 5), p2tog, turn. 45 (49, 53) sts.
Row 43 (43, 45): Sl, k4 (5, 5), p2, sl next 2 sts to cn and hold in front, k2, k2 from cn, k2, p2, k4 (5, 5), k2tog, turn. 44 (48, 52) sts.
Row 44 (44, 46): Sl, p4 (5, 5), k2, p6, k2, p4 (5, 5), p2tog, turn. 43 (47, 51) sts.
Row 45 (45, 47): Sl, k4 (5, 5), p2, k2, sl next 2 sts to cn and hold in back, k2, k2 from cn, p2, k4 (5, 5), k2tog, turn. 42 (46, 50) sts.
Row 46 (46, 48): Sl, p4 (5, 5), k2, p6, k2, p4 (5, 5), p2tog, turn. 41 (45, 49) sts.
Row 47 (47, 49): Sl, k4 (5, 5), p2, sl next 2 sts to cn and hold in front, k2, k2 from cn, p2, k4 (5, 5), k2tog, turn. 40 (44, 48) sts.

Row 48 (48, 50): Sl, p4 (5, 5), k2, p6, k2, p4 (5, 5), p2tog, turn. 39 (43, 47) sts.
Row 49 (49, 51): Sl, k4 (5, 5), p2, k2, sl next 2 sts to cn and hold in back, k2, k2 from cn, p2, k4 (5, 5), k2tog, turn. 38 (42, 46) sts.
Row 50 (50, 52): Sl, p4 (5, 5), k2, p6, k2, p4 (5, 5), p2tog, turn. 37 (41, 45) sts.
Row 51 (51, 53): Sl, k4 (5, 5), p2, sl next 2 sts to cn and hold in front, k2, k2 from cn, p2, k4 (5, 5), k2tog, turn. 36 (40, 44) sts.
Row 52 (52, 54): Sl, p4 (5, 5), k2, p6, k2, p4 (5, 5), p2tog, turn. 35 (39, 43) sts.
Row 53 (53, 55): Sl, k4 (5, 5), p2, sl next 2 sts to cn and hold in back, k2, k2 from cn, p2, k4 (5, 5), k2tog, turn. 34 (38, 42) sts.
Row 54 (54, 56): Sl, p4 (5, 5), k2, p6, k2, p4 (5, 5), p2tog, turn. 33 (37, 41) sts.
Row (55, 57) (two larger sizes only): Sl, k (5, 5), p2, sl next 2 sts to cn and hold in front, k2, k2 from cn, k2, p2, k (5, 5), k2tog, turn. (36, 40) sts.
Row (56, 58) (two larger sizes only): Sl, p (5, 5), k2, p6, k2, p (5, 5), p2tog, turn. (35, 39) sts.
Row (59) (largest size only): Sl, k (5), p2, k2, sl next 2 sts to cn and hold in back, k2, k2 from cn, p2, k (5), k2tog, turn. (38) sts.
Row (60) (largest size only): Sl, p (5), k2, p6, k2, p (5), p2tog, turn. (37) sts.
Row (61) (largest size only): Sl, k (5), p2, sl next 2 sts to cn and hold in front, k2, k2 from cn, p2, k (5), k2tog, turn. (36) sts.
Row (62) (largest size only): Sl, p (5), k2, p6, k2, p (5), p2tog, turn. (35) sts.
Row 55 (57, 63) (all sizes): Sl, p1, k2tog, *p1, k1*, rep. from * to * 7 (8, 8) times, p1, k2tog, turn. 31 (33, 33) sts.
Row 56 (58, 64): Sl, *k1, p1*, rep. from * to * 8 (9, 9) times, k1, p2tog, turn. 30 (32, 32) sts.
Row 57 (59, 65): Sl, *p1, k1*, rep. from * to * 8 (9, 9) times, p1, k2tog, turn. 29 (31, 31) sts.
Row 58 (60, 66): Sl, *k1, p1*, rep. from * to * 8 (9, 9) times, k1, p2tog, turn. 28 (30, 30) sts.
Rep. rows 57 (59, 65) and 58 (60, 66) to row 66 (68, 74). 20 (22, 22) sts.

Neck ruff

Switch to a US 3 (3.25mm) circular needle. Place a marker at the beginning of the round.
Round 67 (69, 75): Sl, *p1, k1*, rep. from * to * 8 (9, 9) times, p1, k2tog, pick up 13 (12, 12) sts on one side of the hat, cast on 7 (7, 7) sts, join to work in the round, being careful not to twist, pick up 13 (12, 12) sts on the other side of the hat. 52 (52, 52) sts.
Rounds 68-77 (70-81, 76-89): K1, p1 rib.
Round 78 (82, 90): K2 (3, 3), yo, k2, yo, k11 (11, 11), yo, k2, yo, k11 (11, 11), yo, k2, yo, k11 (11, 11), yo, k2, yo, k9 (8, 8). 60 (60, 60) sts.

Round 79 (83, 91): K3 (4, 4), yo, k2, yo, k13 (13, 13), yo, k2, yo, k13 (13, 13), yo, k2, yo, k13 (13, 13), yo, k2, yo, k10 (9, 9). 68 (68, 68) sts.
Round 80 (84, 92): K4 (5, 5), yo, k2, yo, k15 (15, 15), yo, k2, yo, k15 (15, 15), yo, k2, yo, k15 (15, 15), yo, k2, yo, k11 (10, 10). 76 (76, 76) sts.
Round 81 (85, 93): K5 (6, 6), yo, k2, yo, k17 (17, 17), yo, k2, yo, k17 (17, 17), yo, k2, yo, k17 (17, 17), yo, k2, yo, k12 (11, 11). 84 (84, 84) sts.
Round 82 (86, 94): K6 (7, 7), yo, k2, yo, k19 (19, 19), yo, k2, yo, k19 (19, 19), yo, k2, yo, k19 (19, 19), yo, k2, yo, k13 (12, 12). 92 (92, 92) sts.
Round 83 (87, 95): K7 (8, 8), yo, k2, yo, k21 (21, 21), yo, k2, yo, k21 (21, 21), yo, k2, yo, k21 (21, 21), yo, k2, yo, k14 (13, 13). 100 (100, 100) sts.
Round (88, 96) (two larger sizes only): K (9, 9), yo, k2, yo, k (23, 23), yo, k2, yo, k (23, 23), yo, k2, yo, k (23, 23), yo, k2, yo, k (14, 14). (108, 108) sts.
Round (89, 97) (two larger sizes only): K (10, 10), yo, k2, yo, k (25, 25), yo, k2, yo, k (25, 25), yo, k2, yo, k (25, 25), yo, k2, yo, k (15, 15). (116, 116) sts.
Round (98) (largest size only): K (11), yo, k2, yo, k (27), yo, k2, yo, k (27), yo, k2, yo, k (27), yo, k2, yo, k (16). (124) sts.
Round (99) (largest size only): K (12), yo, k2, yo, k (29), yo, k2, yo, k (29), yo, k2, yo, k (29), yo, k2, yo, k (17). (132) sts.
Rounds 84-89 (90-95, 100-107) (all sizes):
K2, p2 rib.
Bind off. Weave in ends.

Ears (make 2)

Using a pair of US 3 (3.25mm) needles cast on 25 sts, leaving an 8in./20cm tail for sewing the ears in place.
Rows 1-5: K1, p1 rib.
Cut a tail long enough to weave in. Pull through all 25 stitches and remove them from needle. Pull the tail tightly and secure. Make a strong knot.

FINISHING

1 Sew the ears to the hat in the position shown using an invisible seam.
2 Weave in ends.

A close-up of baby bear's ear

MITTENS

Left mitten cuff

Using US 0 (2mm) double-pointed needles, cast on 24 (28, 28) sts and divide evenly among 3 needles. Join to work in the round, being careful not to twist. Place a marker at the beginning of the round.

Rounds 1-10 (1-12, 1-14): Work in k2, p2 rib.

Thumb gusset

Switch to US 3 (3.25mm) double-pointed needles to work rest of mitten.

Round 1: M1R, k2 (3, 3), p1, k6, p1, k13 (16, 16). 25 (29, 29) sts.

Round 2: K4 (5, 5), p1, k6, p1, k13 (16, 16).

Round 3: M1R, k1, M1L, k1 (2, 2), p1, sl next 2 sts to cn and hold in front, k2, k2 from cn, k2, p1, k13 (16, 16). 27 (31, 31) sts.

Round 4: K6 (7, 7), p1, k6, p1, k13 (16, 16).

Round 5: M1R, k3, M1L, k1 (2, 2), p1, k2, sl next 2 sts to cn and hold in back, k2, k2 from cn, p1, k13 (16, 16). 29 (33, 33) sts.

Round 6: K8 (9, 9), p1, k6, p1, k13 (16, 16).

Round 7: M1R, k5, M1L, k1 (2, 2), p1, sl next 2 sts to cn and hold in front, k2, k2 from cn, k2, p1, k13 (16, 16). 31 (35, 35) sts.

Round 8: K10 (11, 11), p1, k6, p1, k13 (16, 16).

Round 9: M1R, k7, M1L, k1 (2, 2), p1, k2, sl next 2 sts to cn and hold in back, k2, k2 from cn, p1, k13 (16, 16). 33 (37, 37) sts.

Round 10: K1, place 9 (9, 9) thumb stitches on waste yarn and rejoin to work hand stitches in the round, k2 (3, 3), p1, k6, p1, k13 (16, 16). 24 (28, 28) sts.

Round 11: K3 (4, 4), p1, sl next 2 sts to cn and hold in front, k2, k2 from cn, k2, p1, k13 (16, 16).

Round 12: K3 (4, 4), p1, k6, p1, k13 (16, 16).

Round 13: K3 (4, 4), p1, k2, sl next 2 sts to cn and hold in back, k2, k2 from cn, p1, k13 (16, 16).

Round 14: K3 (4, 4), p1, k6, p1, k13 (16, 16).

Round 15: K3 (4, 4), p1, sl next 2 sts to cn and hold in front, k2, k2 from cn, k2, p1, k13 (16, 16).

Round 16: K3 (4, 4), p1, k6, p1, k13 (16, 16).

Round 17: K3 (4, 4), p1, k2, sl next 2 sts to cn and hold in back, k2, k2 from cn, p1, k13 (16, 16).

Round 18: K3 (4, 4), p1, k6, p1, k13 (16, 16).

Round 19: K3 (4, 4), p1, sl next 2 sts to cn and hold in front, k2, k2 from cn, k2, p1, k13 (16, 16).

The cable knit pattern is repeated on the back of the mittens.

Round 20: K3 (4, 4), p1, k6, p1, k13 (16, 16).
Round 21: K3 (4, 4), p1, k2, sl next 2 sts to cn and hold in back, k2, k2 from cn, p1, k13 (16, 16).
Round 22: K3 (4, 4), p1, k6, p1, k13 (16, 16).
Round (23, 23) (two larger sizes only): K (4, 4), p1, sl next 2 sts to cn and hold in front, k2, k2 from cn, k2, p1, k (16, 16).
Round (24, 24) (two larger sizes only): K (4, 4), p1, k6, p1, k (16, 16).
Round (25, 25) (two larger sizes only): K (4, 4), p1, k2, sl next 2 sts to cn and hold in back, k2, k2 from cn, p1, k (16, 16).
Round (26) (largest size only): K (4), p1, k6, p1, k (16).
Round (27) (largest size only): K (4), p1, sl next 2 sts to cn and hold in front, k2, k2 from cn, k2, p1, k (16).
Round (28) (largest size only): K (4), p1, k6, p1, k (16).
Closing up the top
Round 23 (26, 29) (all sizes): K2tog to end of round. 12 (14, 14) sts.
Round 24 (27, 30): Knit.
Round 25 (28, 31): K2tog to end of round. (If you get to the end of the round with only one stitch left, knit it.) 6 (7, 7) sts.
Finish as for Hat ears.

Thumb

Place 9 stitches from waste yarn onto US 3 (3.25mm) double-pointed needles. Rejoin yarn and pick up one extra stitch in the corner where the mitten meets the gusset. Place a marker at the beginning of the round. 10 sts.
Rounds 1-6 (1-6, 1-8): Knit.
Round 7 (7, 9): K2tog to end of round. 5 sts.
Finish as for Hat ears.

Right mitten cuff

Using US 0 (2mm) double-pointed needles, cast on 24 (28, 28) sts and divide evenly among 3 needles. Join to work in the round, being careful not to twist. Place a marker at the beginning of the round.
Rounds 1-10 (1-12, 1-14): Work in k2, p2 rib.

Thumb gusset

Switch to US 3 (3.25mm) double-pointed needles to work rest of mitten.
Round 1: K13 (16, 16), p1, k6, p1, k2 (3, 3), M1R. 25 (29, 29) sts.
Round 2: K13 (16, 16), p1, k6, p1, k4 (5, 5).
Round 3: K13 (16, 16), p1, k2, sl next 2 sts to cn and hold in front, k2, k2 from cn, p1, k1 (2, 2), M1R, k1, M1L. 27 (31, 31) sts.
Round 4: K13 (16, 16), p1, k6, p1, k6 (7, 7).
Round 5: K13 (16, 16), p1, sl next 2 sts to cn and hold in back , k2, k2 from cn, p1, k1 (2, 2), M1R, k3, M1L. 29 (33, 33) sts.
Round 6: K13 (16, 16), p1, k6, p1, k8 (9, 9).
Round 7: K13 (16, 16), p1, k2, sl next 2 sts to cn and hold in front, k2, k2 from cn, p1, k1 (2, 2), M1R, k5, M1L. 31 (35, 35) sts.
Round 8: K13 (16, 16), p1, k6, p1, k10 (11, 11).
Round 9: K13 (16, 16), p1, sl next 2 sts to cn and hold in back, k2, k2 from cn, k2, p1, k1 (2, 2), M1R, k7, M1L. 33 (37, 37) sts.
Round 10: K13 (16, 16), p1, k6, p1, k2 (3, 3), place 9 (9, 9) thumb stitches on waste yarn and rejoin to work hand stitches in the round, k1, 24 (28, 28) sts.

Round 11: K13 (16, 16), p1, k2, sl next 2 sts to cn and hold in front, k2, k2 from cn, p1, k3 (4, 4).
Round 12: K13 (16, 16), p1, k6, p1, k3 (4, 4).
Round 13: K13 (16, 16), p1, sl next 2 sts to cn and hold in back, k2, k2 from cn, k2, p1, k3 (4, 4).
Round 14: K13 (16, 16), p1, k6, p1, k3 (4, 4).
Round 15: K13 (16, 16), p1, k2, sl next 2 sts to cn and hold in front, k2, k2 from cn, p1, k3 (4, 4).
Round 16: K13 (16, 16), p1, k6, p1, k3 (4, 4).
Round 17: K13 (16, 16), p1, sl next 2 sts to cn and hold in back, k2, k2 from cn, k2, p1, k3 (4, 4).
Round 18: K13 (16, 16), p1, k6, p1, k3 (4, 4).
Round 19: K13 (16, 16), p1, k2, sl next 2 sts to cn and hold in front, k2, k2 from cn, p1, k3 (4, 4).
Round 20: K13 (16, 16), p1, k6, p1, k3 (4, 4).
Round 21: K13 (16, 16), p1, sl next 2 sts to cn and hold in back, k2, k2 from cn, k2, p1, k3 (4, 4).
Round 22: K13 (16, 16), p1, k6, p1, k3 (4, 4).
Round (23, 23) (two larger sizes only): K (16, 16), p1, k2, sl next 2 sts to cn and hold in front, k2, k2 from cn, p1, k (4, 4).
Round (24, 24) (two larger sizes only): K (16, 16), p1, k6, p1, k (4, 4).
Round (25, 25) (two larger sizes only): K (16, 16), p1, sl next 2 sts to cn and hold in back, k2, k2 from cn, p1, k (4, 4).
Round (26) (largest size only): K (16), p1, k6, p1, k (4).
Round (27) (largest size only): K (16), p1, k2, sl next 2 sts to cn and hold in front, k2, k2 from cn, p1, k (4).
Round (28) (largest size only): K (16), p1, k6, p1, k (4).
Closing up the top
Round 23 (26, 29) (all sizes): K2tog to end of round. 12 (14, 14) sts.
Round 24 (27, 30): Knit.
Round 25 (28, 31): K2tog to end of round. (If you get to the end of the round with only one stitch left, knit it.) 6 (7, 7) sts.
Finish as for Hat ears.

Thumb

Place 9 stitches from scrap yarn onto US 3 (3.25 mm) double-pointed needles. Rejoin yarn and pick up one extra stitch in the corner where the mitten meets the gusset. Place a marker at the beginning of the round. 10 sts.
Rounds 1-6 (1-6, 1-8): Knit.
Round 7 (7, 9): K2tog to end of round. 5 sts.
Finish as for Hat ears.

little piggy

This little pink piggy is full of character. A simple crocheted spiral makes the snout on the hat and the little mittens are cleverly shaped like piggy feet.

COVERALL HAT AND MITTENS
LEVEL: intermediate
SIZES
6-12 months (12-24 months, 2-3 years)
Finished measurements
From "cheek to cheek" around the hat:
14 (14½, 15)in. (36 [37, 38]cm)
Mitten circumference: 5½ (6, 6½)in. (13.75 [15, 16.25]cm)
Mitten length: 5½ (6.5, 7)in. (14 [16.5, 18] cm)
MATERIALS
HAT
Main yarn:
Color A: 1 x 3oz (85g) ball (135yd/123m) Lion Brand Jiffy Yarn, 100% acrylic, Light Pink
Small amounts:
Color B: Lion Brand Jiffy Yarn, 100% acrylic, Blossom
Color C: Lion Brand Jiffy Yarn, 100% acrylic, Dusty Pink
Color D: Lion Brand Jiffy Yarn, 100% acrylic, Dark Grey Heather
Needles:
• 1 pair of US 3 (3.25mm) needles
• US 3 (3.25mm) circular needles
• 4 x US 3 (3.25mm) double-pointed needles
• Stitch marker
• US C-2 (2.75mm) crochet hook
• Yarn needle
MITTENS
Yarn:
1 x 3oz (85g) ball (135yd/123m) Lion Brand Jiffy Yarn, 100% acrylic, Light Pink
Needles:
• 4 x US 0 (2mm) double-pointed needles
• 4 x US 3 (3.25mm) double-pointed needles
• Yarn needle
GAUGE
16 sts and 25 rows = 4in./10cm square in stockinette stitch worked with US 3 (3.25mm) needles.
19 sts and 28 rows = 4in./10cm square in k1, p1 rib worked with US 3 (3.25mm) needles.

HAT

Using a pair of US 3 (3.25mm) needles and A, cast on 57 (61, 65) sts.
Rows 1-6 (6, 6): K1, p1 rib.
Rows 7- 30 (30, 32): Work in stockinette stitch, starting with a k row.
Row 31 (31, 33): K18 (19, 21), k2tog, k17 (19, 19), k2tog, turn. 55 (59, 63) sts.
Row 32 (32, 34): Sl, p17 (19, 19), p2tog, turn. 54 (58, 62) sts.
Row 33 (33, 35): Sl, k17 (19, 19), k2tog, turn. 53 (57, 61) sts.
Rep. rows 32 (32, 34) and 33 (33, 35) to row 54 (56, 62). 32 (34, 34) sts.
Row 55 (57, 63): Sl, *p1, k1* rep. from * to * 8 (9, 9) times, p1, k2tog, turn. 31 (33, 33) sts.
Row 56 (58, 64): Sl, *k1, p1* rep. from * to * 8 (9, 9) times, k1, p2tog, turn. 30 (32, 32) sts.
Rep. rows 55 (57, 63) and 56 (58, 64) to row 66 (68, 74). 20 (22, 22) sts.

Neck ruff

Switch to US 3 (3.25mm) circular needles. Place a marker at the beginning of the round.
Round 67 (69, 75): Sl, *p1, k1* rep. from * to * 8 (9, 9) times, p1, k2tog, pick up 13 (12, 12) sts on one side of the hat, cast on 7 (7, 7) sts, join to work in the round, being careful not to twist, pick up 13 (12, 12) sts on the other side of the hat. 52 (52, 52) sts.
Rounds 68-77 (70-81, 76-89): K1, p1 rib.
Round 78 (82, 90): K2 (3, 3), yo, k2, yo, k11 (11, 11), yo, k2, yo, k11 (11, 11), yo, k2, yo, k11 (11, 11), yo, k2, yo, k9 (8, 8). 60 (60, 60) sts.
Round 79 (83, 91): K3 (4, 4), yo, k2, yo, k13 (13, 13), yo, k2, yo, k13 (13, 13), yo, k2, yo, k13 (13, 13), yo, k2, yo, k10 (9, 9). 68 (68, 68) sts.
Round 80 (84, 92): K4 (5, 5), yo, k2, yo, k15 (15, 15), yo, k2, yo, k15 (15, 15), yo, k2, yo, k15 (15, 15), yo, k2, yo, k11 (10, 10). 76 (76, 76) sts.
Round 81 (85, 93): K5 (6, 6), yo, k2, yo, k17 (17, 17), yo, k2, yo, k17 (17, 17), yo, k2, yo, k17 (17, 17), yo, k2, yo, k12 (11, 11). 84 (84, 84) sts.
Round 82 (86, 94): K6 (7, 7), yo, k2, yo, k19 (19, 19), yo, k2, yo, k19 (19, 19), yo, k2, yo, k19 (19, 19), yo, k2, yo, k13 (12, 12). 92 (92, 92) sts.
Round 83 (87, 95): K7 (8, 8), yo, k2, yo, k21 (21, 21), yo, k2, yo, k21 (21, 21), yo, k2, yo, k21 (21, 21), yo, k2, yo, k14 (13, 13). 100 (100, 100) sts.
Round (88, 96) (two larger sizes only): K (9, 9), yo, k2, yo, k (23, 23), yo, k2, yo, k (23, 23), yo, k2, yo, k (23, 23), yo, k2, yo, k (14, 14). (108, 108) sts.

The triangular-tipped ears of little piggy.

Round (89, 97) (two larger sizes only): K (10, 10), yo, k2, yo, k (25, 25), yo, k2, yo, k (25, 25), yo, k2, yo, k (25, 25), yo, k2, yo, k (15, 15). (116, 116) sts.

Round (98) (largest size only): K (11), yo, k2, yo, k (27), yo, k2, yo, k (27), yo, k2, yo, k (27), yo, k2, yo, k (16). (124) sts.

Round (99) (largest size only): K (12), yo, k2, yo, k (29), yo, k2, yo, k (29), yo, k2, yo, k (29), yo, k2, yo, k (17). (132) sts.

Rounds 84-89 (90-95, 100-105) (all sizes): K1, p1 rib.

Bind off. Weave in ends.

Ears (make 2)

Using US 3 (3.25mm) double-pointed needles and A, cast on 24 sts, leaving an 8in./20cm tail for sewing the ears in place, and divide evenly among 3 double-pointed needles. Join to work in the round, being careful not to twist.

Round 1-4: Knit.

Round 5: K2tog, k8, k2tog, k2tog, k8, k2tog. 20 sts.

Round 6: K2tog, k6, k2tog, k2tog, k6, k2tog. 16 sts.

Round 7: K2tog, k4, k2tog, k2tog, k4, k2tog. 12 sts.

Round 8: K2tog, k2, k2tog, k2tog, k2, k2tog. 8 sts.

Round 9: K2tog 4 times. 4 sts.

Cut a tail long enough to weave in. Pull through all the stitches. Remove them from the needles. Pull the tail tightly and secure. Weave in ends.

FINISHING

1 Sew the ears to the hat in the position shown using an invisible seam.

2 Weave in ends.

Pig snout

This pattern is crocheted in spiral. Don't join at the end of a row but continue working.

With B, ch6.

Round 1: Skip first chain, sc in each of next 4 ch, 3sc in last ch (turn work so you are working on bottom of chain), sc in next 3 sts, 2sc in last ch. 12 sc.

Round 2: (2sc in next st, sc in each of next 3 sts, 2sc in next st, sc) twice. 16 sc.

Round 3: (2sc in next st, sc in each of next 5 sts, 2sc in next st, sc) twice. 20 sc.

Round 4: (Sc, 2sc in next st, sc in each of next 5 sts, 2sc in next st, sc, 2sc in next st) twice. 26 sc. Sl st in next st and finish off. Leave long enough tail for sewing.

FINISHING

1 Embroider the nostrils in satin stitch using C.

2 Sew the pig snout to the hat in the position shown using an invisible seam.

3 Embroider the eyes in satin stitch using D.

4 Weave in ends.

The combination of knitted ears, a crocheted snout, and embroidered eyes and nostrils complete the face.

MITTENS

(MAKE 2)

Cuff

Using US 0 (2mm) double-pointed needles, cast on 22 (24, 26) sts and divide evenly among 3 needles. Join to work in the round, being careful not to twist. Place a marker at the beginning of the round.
Rounds 1-10 (1-12, 1-14): Work in k1, p1 rib.

Thumb gusset

Switch to US 3 (3.25mm) double-pointed needles to work rest of mitten.
Round 1: M1R, knit to end of round. 23 (25, 27) sts.
Round 2: Knit.
Round 3: M1R, k1, M1L, knit to end of round. 25 (27, 29) sts.
Round 4: Knit.
Round 5: M1R, k3, M1L, knit to end of round. 27 (29, 31) sts.
Round 6: Knit.
Round 7: M1R, k5, M1L, knit to end of round. 29 (31, 33) sts.
Round 8: Knit.
Round (9, 9) (two larger sizes only): M1R, k7, M1L, knit to end of round. (33, 35) sts.
Round 9 (10, 10): K1, place 7 (9, 9) thumb stitches on waste yarn and rejoin to work hand stitches in the round, k21 (23, 25). 22 (24, 26) sts.
Rounds 10-20 (11-24, 11-25): Knit.

Index and middle fingers

Round 21 (25, 26): K6 (6, 7), place next 11 (12, 13) sts to waste yarn, cast on 2 sts, k5 (6, 6). 13 (14, 15) sts.
Round 22 (26, 27-28): Knit.
Round 23 (27, 29): K2tog to end of round. (If you get to the end of the round with only one stitch left, knit it.) 7 (7, 8) sts.
Round 24 (28, 30): Knit.
Finish off as for the Hat ears.

Ring and pinky fingers

Place 11 (12, 13) stitches from waste yarn onto US 3 (3.25mm) double-pointed needles. Rejoin yarn and pick up 2 sts from 2 cast-on sts. Place a marker at the beginning of the round. 13 (14, 15) sts.
Round 21-22 (25-26, 26-28): Knit.
Round 23 (27, 29): K2tog to end of round. (If you get to the end of the round with only one stitch left, knit it.) 7 (7, 8) sts.
Round 24 (28, 30): Knit.
Finish off as for the Hat ears.

Thumb

Place 7 (9, 9) stitches from waste yarn onto US 3 (3.25mm) double-pointed needles. Rejoin yarn and pick up one extra stitch in the corner where the mitten meets the gusset. Place a marker at the beginning of the round. 8 (10, 10) sts.
Rounds 1-6 (1-6, 1-8): Knit.
Round 7 (7, 9): K2tog to end of round. 4 (5, 5) sts.
Finish off as for the Hat ears.

The piggy-trotter shape of the mittens makes them great fun as well as comfortable to wear.

feathered friends

sleepy bluebird

An easy-to-knit beak and some basic embroidery transform this simple project into a stylish set. The hat decoration is repeated smaller on the mittens.

COVERALL HAT AND MITTENS
LEVEL: beginner
SIZES
6-12 months (12-24 months, 2-3 years)
Finished measurements
From "cheek to cheek" around the hat:
14 (14.5, 15)in. (36 [37, 38]cm)
Mitten circumference: 5½ (6, 6½)in.
(13.75 [15, 16.25]cm)
Mitten length: 5½ (6.5, 7)in.
(14 [16.5, 18]cm)
MATERIALS
HAT
Main yarn:
Color A: 1 x 3oz (85g) ball (135yd/123m)
Lion Brand Jiffy Yarn, 100% acrylic,
Pastel Blue
Small amounts:
Color B: Lion Brand Jiffy Yarn, 100%
acrylic, Blossom
Color C: Lion Brand Jiffy Yarn, 100%
acrylic, Black
Needles:
•1 pair of US 3 (3.25mm) needles
•US 3 (3.25mm) circular needle
•4 x US 3 (3.25mm) double-pointed needles
•Stitch marker
•Yarn needle
•Small amount of toy stuffing
MITTENS
Main yarn:
Color A: 1 x 3oz (85g) ball (135yd/123m)
Lion Brand Jiffy Yarn, 100% acrylic,
Pastel Blue
Small amounts:
Color B: Lion Brand Jiffy Yarn, 100%
acrylic, Blossom
Color C: Lion Brand Jiffy Yarn, 100%
acrylic, Black
Needles:
•4 x US 0 (2mm) double-pointed needles
•4 x US 3 (3.25mm) double-pointed needles
•Yarn needle
GAUGE
16 sts and 25 rows = 4in./10cm square
in stockinette stitch worked with US 3
(3.25mm) needles.
19 sts and 28 rows = 4in./10cm square in k1,
p1 rib worked with US 3 (3.25mm) needles.

HAT

Using a pair of US 3 (3.25mm) needles and A, cast on 57 (61, 65) sts.
Rows 1-6 (6, 6): K1, p1 rib.
Rows 7-30 (30, 32): Work in stockinette stitch, starting with a k row.
Row 31 (31, 33): K18 (19, 21), k2tog, k17 (19, 19), k2tog, turn. 55 (59, 63) sts.
Row 32 (32, 34): Sl, p17 (19, 19), p2tog, turn. 54 (58, 62) sts.
Row 33 (33, 35): Sl, k17 (19, 19), k2tog, turn. 53 (57, 61) sts.
Rep. rows 32 (32, 34) and 33 (33, 35) to row 54 (56, 62). 32 (34, 34) sts.
Row 55 (57, 63): Sl, *p1, k1* rep. from * to * 8 (9, 9) times, p1, k2tog, turn. 31 (33, 33) sts.
Row 56 (58, 64): Sl, *k1, p1* rep. from * to * 8 (9, 9) times, k1, p2tog, turn. 30 (32, 32) sts.
Rep. rows 55 (57, 63) and 56 (58, 64) to row 66 (68, 74). 20 (22, 22) sts.

Neck ruff

Switch to a US 3 (3.25mm) circular needle. Place a marker at the beginning of the round.
Round 67 (69, 75): Sl, *p1, k1* rep. from * to * 8 (9, 9) times, p1, k2tog, pick up 13 (12, 12) sts on one side of the hat, cast on 7 (7, 7) sts, join to work in the round, being careful not to twist, pick up 13 (12, 12) sts on the other side of the hat. 52 (52, 52) sts.
Rounds 68-77 (70-81, 76-89): K1, p1 rib.
Round 78 (82, 90): K2 (3, 3), yo, k2, yo, k11 (11, 11), yo, k2, yo, k11 (11, 11), yo, k2, yo, k11 (11, 11), yo, k2, yo, k9 (8, 8). 60 (60, 60) sts.
Round 79 (83, 91): K3 (4, 4), yo, k2, yo, k13 (13, 13), yo, k2, yo, k13 (13, 13), yo, k2, yo, k13 (13, 13), yo, k2, yo, k10 (9, 9). 68 (68, 68) sts.

The beak is lightly stuffed so that it stands up on the hat.

Much of the sleepy bluebird is knitted in k1, p1 rib.

Round 80 (84, 92): K4 (5, 5), yo, k2, yo, k15 (15, 15), yo, k2, yo, k15 (15, 15), yo, k2, yo, k15 (15, 15), yo, k2, yo, k11 (10, 10). 76 (76, 76) sts.

Round 81 (85, 93): K5 (6, 6), yo, k2, yo, k17 (17, 17), yo, k2, yo, k17 (17, 17), yo, k2, yo, k17 (17, 17), yo, k2, yo, k12 (11, 11). 84 (84, 84) sts.

Round 82 (86, 94): K6 (7, 7), yo, k2, yo, k19 (19, 19), yo, k2, yo, k19 (19, 19), yo, k2, yo, k19 (19, 19), yo, k2, yo, k13 (12, 12). 92 (92, 92) sts.

Round 83 (87, 95): K7 (8, 8), yo, k2, yo, k21 (21, 21), yo, k2, yo, k21 (21, 21), yo, k2, yo, k21 (21, 21), yo, k2, yo, k14 (13, 13). 100 (100, 100) sts.

Round (88, 96) (two larger sizes only): K (9, 9), yo, k2, yo, k (23, 23), yo, k2, yo, k (23, 23), yo, k2, yo, k (23, 23), yo, k2, yo, k (14, 14). (108, 108) sts.

Round (89, 97) (two larger sizes only): K (10, 10), yo, k2, yo, k (25, 25), yo, k2, yo, k (25, 25), yo, k2, yo, k (25, 25), yo, k2, yo, k (15, 15). (116, 116) sts.

Round (98) (largest size only): K (11), yo, k2, yo, k (27), yo, k2, yo, k (27), yo, k2, yo, k (27), yo, k2, yo, k (16). (124) sts.

Round (99) (largest size only): K (12), yo, k2, yo, k (29), yo, k2, yo, k (29), yo, k2, yo, k (29), yo, k2, yo, k (17). (132) sts.

Rounds 84-89 (90-95, 100-105) (all sizes): K1, p1 rib.
Bind off. Weave in ends.

Beak

Using the US 3 (3.25mm) double-pointed needles and B, cast on 24 sts, leaving an 8in./20cm tail for sewing the beak in place and divide evenly among the 3 needles. Join to work in the round, being careful not to twist. Place a marker at the beginning of the round.

Rounds 1-4: Knit.
Round 5: K2tog, k8, k2tog, k2tog, k8, k2tog. 20 sts.
Round 6: K2tog, k6, k2tog, k2tog, k6, k2tog. 16 sts.
Round 7: K2tog, k4, k2tog, k2tog, k4, k2tog. 12 sts.
Round 8: K2tog, k2, k2tog, k2tog, k2, k2tog. 8 sts.
Round 9: K2tog 4 times. 4 sts.
Cut a tail long enough to weave in. Pull through all the stitches and remove them from the needles. Pull the tail tightly and secure. Weave in ends.

FINISHING

1 Lightly stuff the beak.
2 Sew the beak onto the hat.
3 Embroider eyes with eyelashes in backstitch using C.

MITTENS

(MAKE 2)

Cuff

Using US 0 (2mm) double-pointed needles and A cast on 22 (24, 26) sts and divide evenly among 3 needles. Join to work in the round, being careful not to twist. Place a marker at the beginning of the round.
Rounds 1-10 (1-12, 1-14): work in k1, p1 rib.

Thumb gusset

Switch to US 3 (3.25mm) double-pointed needles to work rest of mitten.
Round 1: M1R, knit to end of round. 23 (25, 27) sts.
Round 2: Knit.
Round 3: M1R, k1, M1L, knit to end of round. 25 (27, 29) sts.
Round 4: Knit.
Round 5: M1R, k3, M1L, knit to end of round. 27 (29, 31) sts.
Round 6: Knit.
Round 7: M1R, k5, M1L, knit to end of round. 29 (31, 33) sts.
Round 8: Knit.
Round (9, 9) (two larger sizes only): M1R, k7, M1L, knit to end of round. (33, 35) sts.

Round 9 (10, 10): K1, place 7 (9, 9) thumb stitches on waste yarn and rejoin to work hand stitches in the round, k21, (23, 25). 22 (24, 26) sts.
Rounds 10-22 (11-26, 11-28): Knit.
Closing up the top
Round 23 (27, 29): K2tog to end of round. 11 (12, 13) sts.
Round 24 (28, 30): Knit.
Round 25 (29, 31): K2tog to end of round. (If you get to the end of the round with only one stitch left, knit it.) 6 (6, 7) sts.
Cut a tail long enough to weave in. Pull it through all the stitches and remove them from the needles. Pull the tail tightly and secure. Weave in ends.

Thumb

Place 7 (9, 9) stitches from waste yarn onto US 3 (3.25mm) double-pointed needles. Rejoin yarn and pick up one extra stitch in the corner where the mitten meets the gusset. Place a marker at the beginning of the round 8 (10, 10) sts.
Rounds 1-6 (1-6, 1-8): Knit.
Round 7 (7, 9): K2tog to end of round. 4 (5, 5) sts.
Finish as for mitten Closing up the top.

FINISHING

1 Embroider the beak in satin stitch using B.
2 Embroider eyes with eyelashes in backstitch using C.
3 Weave in ends.

Embroider the beak in the center, and then position the eyelashes on either side.

little red rooster

This bright combination is sure to make your child stand out from the crowd. The eyeballs are crocheted in a spiral, and you can stuff them for extra effect.

COVERALL HAT AND MITTENS
LEVEL: intermediate
SIZES
6-12 months (12-24 months, 2-3 years)
Finished measurements
From "cheek to cheek" around the hat:
14 (14½, 15)in. (36 [37, 38]cm)
Mitten circumference: 5½ (6, 6½)in. (13.75 [15, 16.25]cm)
Mitten length: 5½ (6½, 7)in. (14 [16.5, 18]cm)
MATERIALS
HAT
Main yarn:
Color A: 1 x 3oz (85g) ball (135yd/123m) Lion Brand Jiffy Yarn, 100% acrylic, True Red
Small amounts:
Color B: Lion Brand Jiffy Yarn, 100% acrylic, Black
Color C: Lion Brand Jiffy Yarn, 100% acrylic, White
Color D: Lion Brand Baby's First Yarn, 100% acrylic, Honey Bee
Needles:
• 1 pair of US 3 (3.25mm) needles
• US 3 (3.25mm) circular needles
• 4 x US 3 (3.25 mm) double-pointed needles

• Stitch marker
• US C-2 (2.75mm) crochet hook
• Yarn needle
• Small amount of toy stuffing
MITTENS
Main yarn:
Color A: Lion Brand Jiffy Yarn, 100% acrylic, True Red (2oz [55g], 87yd [80m])
Small amounts:
Color B: Lion Brand Jiffy Yarn, 100% acrylic, Black
Color C: Lion Brand Jiffy Yarn, 100% acrylic, White
Color D: Lion Brand Baby's First Yarn, 100% acrylic, Honey Bee
Needles:
• 4 x US 0 (2mm) double-pointed needles
• 4 x US 3 (3.25mm) double-pointed needles
• US C-2 (2.75mm) crochet hook
• Yarn needle
GAUGE
16 sts and 25 rows = 4in./10cm square in stockinette stitch worked with US 3 (3.25mm) needles.
19 sts and 28 rows = 4in./10cm square in k1, p1 rib worked with US 3 (3.25mm) needles.

HAT

Using a pair of US 3 (3.25mm) needles and B, cast on 57 (61, 65) sts.
Rows 1-6 (6, 6): K1, p1 rib.
Switch to A.
Rows 7- 30 (30, 32): Work in stockinette stitch, starting with a k row.
Row 31 (31, 33): K18 (19, 21), k2tog, k17 (19, 19), k2tog, turn. 55 (59, 63) sts.
Row 32 (32, 34): Sl, p17 (19, 19), p2tog, turn. 54 (58, 62) sts.
Row 33 (33, 35): Sl, k17 (19, 19), k2tog, turn. 53 (57, 61) sts.
Rep. rows 32 (32, 34) and 33 (33, 35) to row 54 (56, 62). 32 (34, 34) sts.
Row 55 (57, 63): Sl, *p1, k1* rep. from * to * 8 (9, 9) times, p1, k2tog, turn. 31 (33, 33) sts.
Row 56 (58, 64): Sl, *k1, p1* rep. from * to * 8 (9, 9) times, k1, p2tog, turn. 30 (32, 32) sts.
Rep. rows 55 (57, 63) and 56 (58, 64) to row 66 (68, 74). 20 (22, 22) sts.

Neck ruff

Switch to US 3 (3.25mm) circular needles. Place a marker at the beginning of the round.
Round 67 (69, 75): Sl, *p1, k1* rep. from * to * 8 (9, 9) times, p1, k2tog, pick up 13 (12, 12) sts on one side of the hat, cast on 7 (7, 7) sts, join to work in the round, being careful not to twist, pick

Little red rooster is made in vibrant red, black, white, and yellow.

up 13 (12, 12) sts on the other side of the hat. 52 (52, 52) sts.

Rounds 68-77 (70-81, 76-89): K1, p1 rib.

Round 78 (82, 90): K2 (3, 3), yo, k2, yo, k11 (11, 11), yo, k2, yo, k11 (11, 11), yo, k2, yo, k11 (11, 11), yo, k2, yo, k9 (8, 8). 60 (60, 60) sts.

Round 79 (83, 91): K3 (4, 4), yo, k2, yo, k13 (13, 13), yo, k2, yo, k13 (13, 13), yo, k2, yo, k13 (13, 13), yo, k2, yo, k10 (9, 9). 68 (68, 68) sts.

Round 80 (84, 92): K4 (5, 5), yo, k2, yo, k15 (15, 15), yo, k2, yo, k15 (15, 15), yo, k2, yo, k15 (15, 15), yo, k2, yo, k11 (10, 10). 76 (76, 76) sts.

Round 81 (85, 93): K5 (6, 6), yo, k2, yo, k17 (17, 17), yo, k2, yo, k17 (17, 17), yo, k2, yo, k17 (17, 17), yo, k2, yo, k12 (11, 11). 84 (84, 84) sts.

Round 82 (86, 94): K6 (7, 7), yo, k2, yo, k19 (19, 19), yo, k2, yo, k19 (19, 19), yo, k2, yo, k19 (19, 19), yo, k2, yo, k13 (12, 12). 92 (92, 92) sts.

Round 83 (87, 95): K7 (8, 8), yo, k2, yo, k21 (21, 21), yo, k2, yo, k21 (21, 21), yo, k2, yo, k21 (21, 21), yo, k2, yo, k14 (13, 13). 100 (100, 100) sts.

Round (88, 96) (two larger sizes only): K (9, 9), yo, k2, yo, k (23, 23), yo, k2, yo, k (23, 23), yo, k2, yo, k (23, 23), yo, k2, yo, k (14, 14). (108, 108) sts.

Round (89, 97) (two larger sizes only): K (10, 10), yo, k2, yo, k (25, 25), yo, k2, yo, k (25, 25), yo, k2, yo, k (25, 25), yo, k2, yo, k (15, 15). (116, 116) sts.

Round (98) (largest size only): K (11), yo, k2, yo, k (27), yo, k2, yo, k (27), yo, k2, yo, k (27), yo, k2, yo, k (16). (124) sts.

Round (99) (largest size only): K (12), yo, k2, yo, k (29), yo, k2, yo, k (29), yo, k2, yo, k (29), yo, k2, yo, k (17). (132) sts.

Rounds 84-89 (90-95, 100-105) (all sizes): K1, p1 rib.
Bind off. Weave in ends.

Eyeballs (make 2)

This pattern is crocheted in spiral. Don't join at the end of a row but continue working.
With US C-2 (2.75mm) crochet hook and C, ch4. Join with sl st to form ring.

Round 1: 7sc through ring.
Round 2: 2sc in each sc. 14 sc.
Round 3: 14sc.
Round 4: 14sc.
End with sl st in next st to join.
Fasten off, leaving a tail long enough for sewing.

Pupils (make 2)

With US C-2 (2.75mm) crochet hook and B, ch4. Join with sl st to form ring.
Round 1: 7sc through ring.
End with sl st in next st to join.
Fasten off, leaving a tail long enough for sewing.

FINISHING

1 Sew pupil onto the eyeball.
2 With C embroider two small pupils (highlights) in satin stitch.
3 Tuck the loose yarn ends into the dome of the eyeball, and a tiny bit of stuffing if you want.
4 Sew eyes onto the hat.
5 Weave in ends.

The integrated hat and neck ruff make these hats so comfortable to wear.

Beak

Using US 3 (3.25mm) double-pointed needles and D, cast on 16 sts, leaving an 8in./20cm tail for sewing the ears in place, and divide evenly among 3 double-pointed needles. Join to work in the round, being careful not to twist. Place a marker at the beginning of the round.

Round 1: Knit.
Round 2: K2tog, k4, k2tog, k2tog, k4, k2tog. 12 sts.
Round 3: Knit.
Round 4: K2tog, k2, k2tog, k2tog, k2, k2tog. 8 sts.
Round 5: Knit.
Round 6: K2tog 4 times. 4 sts.

Cut a tail long enough to weave in. Pull through all 4 stitches and remove them from the needles. Pull the tail tightly and secure. Weave in end. Sew the beak onto the hat.

Head crest

Using a pair of US 3 (3.25mm) needles and A, cast on 3 sts, leaving an 8in./20cm tail for sewing the head crest in place.

Row 1: K1, yo, k1, yo, k1. 5 sts.
Row 2: P2, yo, p1, yo, p2. 7 sts.
Row 3: K3, yo, k1, yo, k3. 9 sts.
Row 4: P4, yo, p1, yo, p4. 11 sts.
Row 5: K5, yo, k1, yo, k5. 13 sts.
Row 6: P6, yo, p1, yo, p6. 15 sts.

Close crest (see page 139 for diagrams)
Row 7: K2, sl next 5 sts, fold right hand and left hand needles parallel to each other with wrong sides facing and points facing to the right (right needle is at the back), slip next st onto a crochet hook; it will be the 8th st in row.

Insert crochet hook into 7th st (from the right needle) and pull this through the loop on hook. Continue in this way:
**pull next st from the left needle through st on hook,
pull next st from right needle through st on hook. **
Rep. from ** to ** until the last slipped st on the right needle has been pulled through the next st on the left needle, pull next st from the left needle through st on hook, slip this st back onto the left needle, unfold needles and hold normally, yo, k1, yo, k2. 7 sts.

Row 8: P3, yo, p1, yo, p3. 9 sts.
Row 9: K4, yo, k1, yo, k4. 11 sts.
Row 10: P5, yo, p1, yo, p5. 13 sts.
Row 11: K6, yo, k1, yo, k6. 15 sts.
Row 12: P7, yo, p1, yo, p7. 17 sts.
Row 13: K8, yo, k1, yo, k8. 19 sts.
Row 14: P9, yo, p1, yo, p9. 21 sts.

Close crest (see page 139 for diagrams)
Row 15: K2, sl next 8 sts, fold right hand and left hand needles parallel to each other with wrong sides facing and points facing to the right (right needle is at the back), slip next st onto a crochet hook; it will be the 11th st in row.

Insert crochet hook into 10th st (from the right needle) and pull this through the loop on hook. Continue in this way:
**pull next st from the left needle through st on hook, pull next st from right needle through st on hook. **

The googly eyes, crest, and beak give this hat its special character.

Fan-fold the head crest as shown here before sewing it to the hat.

Rep. from ** to ** until the last slipped st on the right needle has been pulled through the next st on the left needle, pull next st from the left needle through st on hook, slip this st back onto the left needle, unfold needles and hold normally, yo, k1, yo, k2. 7 sts.

Row 16: P3, yo, p1, yo, p3. 9sts.
Row 17: K4, yo, k1, yo, k4. 11sts.
Row 18: P5, yo, p1, yo, p5. 13 sts.
Row 19: K6, yo, k1, yo, k6. 15 sts.
Row 20: P7, yo, p1, yo, p7. 17 sts.
Row 21: K8, yo, k1, yo, k8. 19 sts.
Row 22: P9, yo, p1, yo, p9. 21 sts.
Close crest (see page 139 for diagrams)
Row 23: Slip next 10 sts, fold right-hand and left-hand needles parallel to each other with wrong sides facing and points facing to the right (right needle is at the back), slip next st onto a crochet hook; it will be the 11th st in row.
Insert crochet hook into 10th st (from the right needle) and pull this through the loop on hook. Continue in this way:
**pull next st from the left needle through st on hook,

pull next st from right needle through st on hook. **
Rep. from ** to ** until the last slipped st on the right needle has been pulled through the next st on the left needle, pull next st from the left needle through st on hook.
Cut a tail long enough to sew in place. Pull through last st. Pull the tail tightly and secure. Weave in end.

FINISHING
1 Fan-fold the head crest, folllowing the photo above.
2 Sew the head crest onto the hat.
3 Weave in ends.

MITTENS

(MAKE 2)

Cuff

Using US 0 (2mm) double-pointed needles and A, cast on 22 (24, 26) sts and divide evenly among 3 needles. Join to work in the round, being careful not to twist. Place a marker at the beginning of the round.
Rounds 1–10 (1–12, 1–14): Work in k1, p1 rib.

Thumb gusset

Switch to US 3 (3.25mm) double-pointed needles to work rest of mitten.
Round 1: M1R, knit to end of round. 23 (25, 27) sts.
Round 2: Knit.
Round 3: M1R, k1, M1L, knit to end of round. 25 (27, 29) sts.
Round 4: Knit.
Round 5: M1R, k3, M1L, knit to end of round. 27 (29, 31) sts.
Round 6: Knit.
Round 7: M1R, k5, M1L, knit to end of round. 29 (31, 33) sts.
Round 8: Knit.
Round (9, 9) (two larger sizes only): M1R, k7, M1L, knit to end of round. (33, 35) sts.
Round 9 (10, 10): K1, place 7 (9, 9) thumb stitches on waste yarn. Rejoin to work hand stitches in the round, k21 (23, 25). 22 (24, 26) sts.
Rounds 10–18 (11–22, 11–24): Knit.
Switch to B.
Rounds 19–22 (23–26, 25–28): Knit.
Closing up the top
Round 23 (27, 29): K2tog to end of round. 11 (12, 13) sts.
Round 24 (28, 30): Knit.
Round 25 (29, 31): K2tog to end of round. (If you get to the end of the round with only one stitch left, knit it.) 6 (6, 7) sts.
Cut a tail long enough to weave in. Pull it through all the stitches and remove them from the needles. Pull the tail tightly and secure. Weave in ends.

Thumb

Place 7 (9, 9) stitches from waste yarn onto US 3 (3.25mm) double-pointed needles. Rejoin yarn and pick up one extra stitch in the corner where the mitten meets the gusset. Place a marker at the beginning of the round. 8 (10, 10) sts.
Rounds 1–6 (1–6, 1–8): Knit.
Round 7 (7, 9): K2tog to end of round. 4 (5, 5) sts.
Finish as for Mitten Closing up the top.

Eyes (make 4)

With US C-2 (2.75mm) crochet hook and C, ch5. Join with sl st to form ring.
Round 1: Ch4, 10hdc in ring, join with sl st on top of the first 4ch stitches. 11hdc.
Finish off, leaving a long tail for sewing.

FINISHING

1 With B, embroider the pupils in the middle of the eyes in satin stitch.
2 Sew the eyes onto the mittens.
3 Weave in ends.

Small bird's beak (make 2)

With D, ch4, 1sl st in 2nd ch from hook, 1sc in 3rd ch from hook, 1hdc in 4th ch from hook.
Finish off, leaving a long tail for sewing.

FINISHING

1 Sew the beak onto the mittens.
2 Weave in ends.

Head crest (make 2)

With A, ch10, 1sl st in first ch, ch15, 1sl st in first ch, ch10, 1sl st in first ch.
Finish off, leaving a long tail for sewing.

FINISHING

1 Sew the head crests onto the mittens.
2 Weave in ends.

The mittens have the same head crest, eyes, and beak as the hat.

cheeky chicken

The cheeky chicken coverall hat is soft and cozy. The head crest on the hat and mittens is knitted, and a little simple crochet is required for the beak.

COVERALL HAT AND MITTENS
LEVEL: intermediate
SIZES
6-12 months (12-24 months, 2-3 years)
Finished measurements
From "cheek to cheek" around the hat:
14 (14½, 15)in. (36 [37, 38]cm)
Mitten circumference: 5½ (6, 6½)in.
(13.75 [15, 16.25]cm)
Mitten length: 5½ (6½, 7)in.
(14 [16.5, 18]cm)
MATERIALS
HAT
Main yarn:
Color A: 1 x 3oz (85g) ball (135yd/123m)
Lion Brand Jiffy Yarn, 100% acrylic, White
Small amounts:
Color B: Lion Brand Jiffy Yarn, 100% acrylic, True Red
Color C: Lion Brand Jiffy Yarn, 100% acrylic, Black
Color D: Lion Brand Baby's First Yarn, 100% acrylic, Honey Bee
Needles:
• 1 pair of US 3 (3.25mm) needles
• US 3 (3.25mm) circular needle
• Stitch marker
• US C-2 (2.75mm) crochet hook
• Yarn needle
MITTENS
Main yarn:
Color A: 1 x 3oz (85g) ball (135yd/123m)
Lion Brand Jiffy Yarn, 100% acrylic, White
Small amounts:
Color B: Lion Brand Jiffy Yarn, 100% acrylic, True Red
Color C: Lion Brand Jiffy Yarn, 100% acrylic, Black
Color D: Lion Brand Baby's First Yarn, 100% acrylic, Honey Bee
Needles:
• 4 x US 0 (2mm) double-pointed needles
• 4 x US 3 (3.25mm) double-pointed needles
• US C-2 (2.75mm) crochet hook
• Yarn needle
GAUGE
16 sts and 25 rows = 4in./10cm square in stockinette stitch, worked with US 3 (3.25mm) needles.
19 sts and 28 rows = 4in./10cm square in k1, p1 rib, worked with US 3 (3.25mm) needles.

The distinctive features of the cheeky chicken are visible from all angles.

HAT

Using a pair of US 3 (3.25mm) needles and A, cast on 57 (61, 65) sts.
Rows 1-6 (6, 6): K1, p1 rib.
Rows 7- 30 (30, 32): Work in stockinette stitch, starting with a k row.
Row 31 (31, 33): K18 (19, 21), k2tog, k17 (19, 19), k2tog, turn. 55 (59, 63) sts.
Row 32 (32, 34): Sl, p17 (19, 19), p2tog, turn. 54 (58, 62) sts.
Row 33 (33, 35): Sl, k17 (19, 19), k2tog, turn. 53 (57, 61) sts.
Rep. rows 32 (32, 34) and 33 (33, 35) to row 54 (56, 62). 32 (34, 34) sts.
Row 55 (57, 63): Sl, *p1, k1* rep. from * to * 8 (9, 9) times, p1, k2tog, turn. 31 (33, 33) sts.
Row 56 (58, 64): Sl, *k1, p1* rep. from * to * 8 (9, 9) times, k1, p2tog, turn. 30 (32, 32) sts.
Rep. rows 55 (57, 63) and 56 (58, 64) to row 66 (68, 74). 20 (22, 22) sts.

Neck ruff

Switch to a US 3 (3.25mm) circular needle. Place a marker at the beginning of the round.

Round 67 (69, 75): Sl, *p1, k1* rep. from * to * 8 (9, 9) times, p1, k2tog, pick up 13 (12, 12) sts on one side of the hat, cast on 7 (7, 7) sts, join to work in the round, being careful not to twist, pick up 13 (12, 12) sts on the other side of the hat. 52 (52, 52) sts.

Rounds 68-77 (70-81, 76-89): K1, p1 rib.

Round 78 (82, 90): K2 (3, 3), yo, k2, yo, k11 (11, 11), yo, k2, yo, k11 (11, 11), yo, k2, yo, k11 (11, 11), yo, k2, yo, k9 (8, 8). 60 (60, 60) sts.

Round 79 (83, 91): K3 (4, 4), yo, k2, yo, k13 (13, 13), yo, k2, yo, k13 (13, 13), yo, k2, yo, k13 (13, 13), yo, k2, yo, k10 (9, 9). 68 (68, 68) sts.

Round 80 (84, 92): K4 (5, 5), yo, k2, yo, k15 (15, 15), yo, k2, yo, k15 (15, 15), yo, k2, yo, k15 (15, 15), yo, k2, yo, k11 (10, 10). 76 (76, 76) sts.

Round 81 (85, 93): K5 (6, 6), yo, k2, yo, k17 (17, 17), yo, k2, yo, k17 (17, 17), yo, k2, yo, k17 (17, 17), yo, k2, yo, k12 (11, 11). 84 (84, 84) sts.

Round 82 (86, 94): K6 (7, 7), yo, k2, yo, k19 (19, 19), yo, k2, yo, k19 (19, 19), yo, k2, yo, k19 (19, 19), yo, k2, yo, k13 (12, 12). 92 (92, 92) sts.

Round 83 (87, 95): K7 (8, 8), yo, k2, yo, k21 (21, 21), yo, k2, yo, k21 (21, 21), yo, k2, yo, k21 (21, 21), yo, k2, yo, k14 (13, 13). 100 (100, 100) sts.

Round (88, 96) (two larger sizes only): K (9, 9), yo, k2, yo, k (23, 23), yo, k2, yo, k (23, 23), yo, k2, yo, k (23, 23), yo, k2, yo, k (14, 14). (108, 108) sts.

Round (89, 97) (two larger sizes only): K (10, 10), yo, k2, yo, k (25, 25), yo, k2, yo, k (25, 25), yo, k2, yo, k (25, 25), yo, k2, yo, k (15, 15). (116, 116) sts.

Round (98) (two larger sizes only): K (11), yo, k2, yo, k (27), yo, k2, yo, k (27), yo, k2, yo, k (27), yo, k2, yo, k (16). (124) sts.

Round (99) (two larger sizes only): K (12), yo, k2, yo, k (29), yo, k2, yo, k (29), yo, k2, yo, k (29), yo, k2, yo, k (17). (132) sts.

Rounds 84-89 (all sizes): (90-95, 100-105): K1, p1 rib.
Bind off. Weave in ends.

Head crest

Using a pair of US 3 (3.25mm) needles and B, cast on 30 sts.

Row 1: Knit.
Row 2: *K1, k2tog* 10 times. 20 sts.
Row 3: *K1, k2tog* 6 times, k2. 14 sts.
Row 4: *K1, k2tog* 4 times, k2. 10 sts.
Row 5: *K1, k2tog* 3 times, k1. 7 sts.
Bind off.

Make sure that you attach the beak and crest as shown here, and embroider the eyes as indicated.

Beak

With US C-2 (2.75mm) crochet hook and D: Ch6, 1sl st in 2nd ch from hook, 1sc in 3rd ch from hook, 1hdc in 4th ch from hook, 1hdc in 5th ch from hook, 1dc in 6th ch from hook, 5ch, 1sl st in 2nd ch from hook, 1sc in 3rd ch from hook, 1hdc in 4th ch from hook, 1dc in 5th ch from hook. Fasten off, leaving a tail long enough for sewing.

FINISHING

1 Sew the beak onto the hat.
2 Sew the head crest onto the hat.
3 Using C, embroider 2 small eyes in satin stitch.
4 Weave in ends.

MITTENS

(MAKE 2)

Cuff

Using US 0 (2mm) double-pointed needles and A, cast on 22 (24, 26) sts and divide evenly among 3 needles. Join to work in the round, being careful not to twist. Place a marker at the beginning of the round.
Rounds 1-10 (1-12, 1-14): Work in k1, p1 rib.

Thumb gusset

Switch to US 3 (3.25mm) double-pointed needles to work rest of mitten.
Round 1: M1R, knit to end of round. 23 (25, 27) sts.
Round 2: Knit.
Round 3: M1R, k1, M1L, knit to end of round. 25 (27, 29) sts.
Round 4: Knit.
Round 5: M1R, k3, M1L, knit to end of round. 27 (29, 31) sts.
Round 6: Knit.
Round 7: M1R, k5, M1L, knit to end of round. 29 (31, 33) sts.
Round 8: Knit.
Round (9, 9) (two larger sizes only): M1R, k7, M1L, knit to end of round. (33, 35) sts.
Round 9 (10, 10): K1, place 7 (9, 9) thumb stitches on waste yarn and rejoin to work hand stitches in the round, k21 (23, 25). 22 (24, 26) sts.
Rounds 10-22 (11-26, 11-28): Knit.
Closing up the top
Round 23 (27, 29): K2tog to end of round. 11 (12, 13) sts.
Round 24 (28, 30): Knit.
Round 25 (29, 31): K2tog to end of round. (If you get to the end of the round with only one stitch left, knit it.) 6 (6, 7) sts.
Cut a tail long enough to weave in. Pull it through all the stitches and remove them from the needles. Pull the tail tightly and secure. Weave in ends.

Thumb

Place 7 (9, 9) stitches from waste yarn onto US 3 (3.25mm) double-pointed needles. Rejoin yarn and pick up one extra stitch in the corner where the mitten meets the gusset. Place a marker at the beginning of the round. 8 (10, 10) sts.
Rounds 1-6 (1-6, 1-8): Knit.
Round 7 (9, 9): K2tog to end of round. 4 (5, 5) sts.
Finish as for mitten Closing up the top.

Head crest

Using a pair of US 3 (3.25mm) needles and B, cast on 20 sts.
Row 1: Knit.
Row 2: K2tog to end of row. 10 sts.
Row 3: Knit.
Row 4: K2tog to end of row. 5 sts.
Row 5: Knit.
Bind off.

Beak

With US C-2 (2.75mm) crochet hook and D: Ch5, 1sl st in 2nd ch from hook, 1sc in 3rd ch from hook, 1hdc in 4th ch from hook, 1dc in 5th ch from hook, ch4, 1sl st in 2nd ch from hook, 1sc in 3rd ch from hook, 1hdc in 4th ch from hook. Fasten off.

FINISHING

1 Sew the beak onto the mittens.
2 Sew the head crest onto the mittens.
3 Using C, embroider the eyes in satin stitch.
4 Weave in ends.

Each mitten has its own crest, beak, and eyes.

wise owl

Children are sure to love the large eyes and pointed ears of wise owl. The hat is secured with a fastener, and the scarf will keep little necks cozy and warm.

HAT, MITTENS, AND SCARF
LEVEL: advanced
SIZES
6-12 months (12-24 months, 2-3 years)
Finished measurements
From "cheek to cheek" around the hat:
14 (14½, 15)in. (36 [37, 38]cm)
Mitten circumference: 5½ (6, 6½)in.
(1375 [15, 16.25]cm)
Mitten length: 5½ (6½, 7)in. (14 [16.5, 18]cm)
Scarf length: 37in. (94cm)
Scarf width: 3in. (7.5cm)
MATERIALS
HAT
Main yarn:
Color A: 1 x 3oz (85g) ball (135yd/123m) Lion Brand Jiffy Yarn, 100% acrylic, Dark Grey Heather
Small amounts:
Color B: Lion Brand Jiffy Yarn, 100% acrylic, White
Color C: Lion Brand Jiffy Yarn, 100% acrylic, Black
Color D: Lion Brand Jiffy Yarn, 100% acrylic, Taupe Mist
Color E: Lion Brand Jiffy Yarn, 100% acrylic, Rust
Needles:
•1 pair of US 3 (3.25mm) needles
•Stitch marker
•US C-2 (2.75mm) crochet hook
•Yarn needle
•Small amount of toy stuffing
MITTENS
Main yarn:
Color A: 1 x 3oz (85g) ball (135yd/123m) Lion Brand Jiffy Yarn, 100% acrylic, Dark Grey Heather

Small amounts:
Color B: Lion Brand Jiffy Yarn, 100% acrylic, White
Color C: Lion Brand Jiffy Yarn, 100% acrylic, Black
Color D: Lion Brand Jiffy Yarn, 100% acrylic, Taupe Mist
Color E: Lion Brand Jiffy Yarn, 100% acrylic, Rust
Needles:
•4 x US 0 (2mm) double-pointed needles
•4 x US 3 (3.25mm) double-pointed needles
•US C-2 (2.75mm) crochet hook
•Yarn needle
SCARF
Main yarn:
Color D: 1 x 3oz (85g) ball (135yd/123m) Lion Brand Jiffy Yarn, 100% acrylic, Taupe Mist
Small amounts:
Color F: Lion Brand Jiffy Yarn, 100% acrylic, Green Tea
Color G: Lion Brand Jiffy Yarn, 100% acrylic, Apple Green
Color H: Lion Brand Jiffy Yarn, 100% acrylic, Grass Green
Color I: Lion Brand Jiffy Yarn, 100% acrylic, Avocado
Needles:
•1 pair of US 3 (3.25mm) needles
•Yarn needle
GAUGE
16 sts and 25 rows = 4in./10cm square in stockinette stitch, worked with US 3 (3.25mm) needles.
19 sts and 28 rows = 4in./10cm square in k1, p1 rib, worked with US 3 (3.25mm) needles.

HAT

Using a pair of US 3 (3.25mm) needles and A, cast on 57 (61, 65) sts. Place a stitch marker at the beginning of the row.
Rows 1-6 (6, 6): K1, p1 rib.
Row 7: Knit.
Row 8: K6 (6, 6), p45 (49, 53), k6 (6, 6).
Rep. rows 7 and 8 to row 20 (20, 22).
Row 21 (21, 23): K19 (20, 22), yo, k1, yo, k17 (19, 19), yo, k1, yo, k19 (20, 22). 61 (65, 69) sts.
Row 22 (22, 24): K6 (6, 6), p14 (15, 17), yo, p1, yo, p19 (21, 21), yo, p1, yo, p14 (15, 17), k6 (6, 6). 65 (69, 73) sts.
Row 23 (23, 25): K21 (22, 24), yo, k1, yo, k21 (23, 23), yo, k1, yo, k21 (22, 24). 69 (73, 77) sts.
Row 24 (24, 26): K6 (6, 6), p16 (17, 19), yo, p1. yo, p23 (25, 25), yo, p1, yo, p16 (17, 19), k6 (6, 6). 73 (77, 81) sts.
Row 25 (25, 27): K23 (24, 26), yo, k1, yo, k25 (27, 27), yo, k1, yo, k23 (24, 26). 77 (81, 85) sts.
Row 26 (26, 28): K6 (6, 6), p18 (19, 21), yo, p1, yo, p27 (29, 29), yo, p1, yo, p18 (19, 21), k6 (6, 6). 81 (85, 89) sts.
Row 27 (27, 29): K25 (26, 28), yo, k1, yo, k29 (31, 31), yo, k1, yo, k25 (26, 28). 85 (89, 93) sts.
Row 28 (28, 30): K6 (6, 6), p20 (21, 23), yo, p1, yo, p31 (33, 33), yo, p1, yo, p20 (21, 23), k6 (6, 6). 89 (93, 97) sts.
Row 29 (29, 31): K27 (28, 30), yo, k1, yo, k33 (35, 35), yo, k1, yo, k27 (28, 30). 93 (97, 101) sts.
Row 30 (30, 32): K6 (6, 6), p22 (23, 25), yo, p1, yo, p35 (37, 37), yo, p1, yo, p22 (23, 25), k6 (6, 6). 97 (101, 105) sts.
Close ears (see page 139 for diagrams)
Row 31 (31, 33): K18 (19, 21), sl next 11 (11, 11) sts, fold right-hand and left-hand needles parallel to each other with wrong sides together and points facing to the right (right needle is at the back), slip next st onto a crochet hook; it will be the 30th (31st, 33rd) st in row.
Insert crochet hook into 29th (30th, 32nd) st (from the right needle) and pull this through the loop on the hook. Continue in this way:
**pull next st from the left needle through st on hook,
pull next st from the right needle through st on hook,**
Rep. from ** to ** until the last slipped st on the right needle has been pulled through the next st on the left needle, pull next st from the left needle through st on hook, slip this st back onto the left needle, unfold needles and hold normally, slip 19th (20th, 22nd) st from right

The hat will overlap the scarf, proving just as cozy as a coverall hat.

needle to left needle, k2tog, k17 (19, 19), sl next 10 (10, 10) sts, fold right-hand and left-hand needles parallel to each other with wrong sides together and points facing to the right (right needle is at the back), slip next st onto a crochet hook; it will be 47th (50th, 52nd) st in row.
Insert crochet hook into 46th (49th, 51st) st (from the right needle) and pull this through the loop on the hook. Continue in this way:
**pull next st from the left needle through st on hook,
pull next st from the right needle through st on hook,**
Rep. from ** to ** until the last slipped st on the right needle has been pulled through the next st on the left needle, pull next st from the left needle through st on hook, slip this st back onto the left needle, unfold needles and hold normally, k2tog, turn. 55 (59, 63) sts.
Row 32 (32, 34): Sl, p17 (19, 19), p2tog, turn. 54 (58, 62) sts.
Row 33 (33, 35): Sl, k17 (19, 19), k2tog, turn. 53 (57, 61) sts.
Rep. rows 32 (32, 34) and 33 (33, 35) to row 54 (58, 64). 32 (32, 32) sts.
Row 55 (59, 65): Sl, *p1, k1* rep. from * to * 8 (9, 9) times, p1, k2tog, turn. 31 (31, 31) sts.
Row 56 (60, 66): Sl, *k1, p1* rep. from * to * 8 (9, 9) times, k1, p2tog, turn. 30 (30, 30) sts.
Rep. rows 55 (59, 65) and 56 (60, 66) to row 66 (68, 74). 20 (22, 22) sts.
Cut yarn, leaving a long enough tail to weave in. Leave 20 (22, 22) sts on the needle.

Fastener

Rejoin the yarn at marker, push the crochet hook through at the marker from front to back and ch15.

1hdc in 5th ch from hook, 1hdc in next ch, ch2, skip 2 ch, 1hdc in each of next 6 ch, with right side facing insert hook into edge of rib row 3 and work 1sc, work a further 14 (14, 15) sc along bottom edge of hat (approximately in each alternate row) to sts held on needle, taking the sts off the needle one at a time work 1sc into each of the 20 (22, 22) sts, work a further 15 (15, 16) sc along bottom edge of hat (approximately in each alternate row) to front edge.
Fasten off. Weave in ends.

Eyes (make 2)

This pattern is crocheted in spiral. Don't join at the end of a row but continue working.
With the crochet hook and B: Ch4. Join with sl st to form ring.
Round 1: ch1, 9hdc through ring.
Round 2: 2hdc in each hdc. 20ch.
Round 3: 1hdc in each hdc. 20ch.
End with sl st in next st to join. Fasten off, leaving a tail long enough for sewing.

Eye edging (make 2)

With the crochet hook and D: Ch20. Join with sl st to form ring.
Round 1: ch1, 1hdc in each ch. 20hdc.
End with sl st in next st to join. Fasten off, leaving a tail long enough for sewing.

Pupils (make 2)

With the crochet hook and C: Ch4. Join with sl st to form ring.
Round 1: 7sc through ring.
End with sl st in next st to join.
Fasten off, leaving a tail long enough for sewing.

The knitted strap is fastened with a simple crocheted button.

Beak

With the crochet hook and E: Ch7.
1 sl st in 2nd ch from hook, 1sc in 3rd ch from hook, 1hdc in 4th ch from hook, 1dc in 5th ch from hook, 1dc in 6th ch from hook. Fasten off.

Button

With the crochet hook and E: Ch3. Join with sl st to form ring.
Round 1: 5sc through ring.
End with sl st in next st to join, leaving an 8in./20cm tail for sewing the button in place. Using a yarn needle or crochet hook, pull the tail through all 5 stitches. Pull the tail tightly and secure. Make a strong knot.

FINISHING

1 Sew the pupils onto the eyes.
2 With B embroider two small highlights on pupils in satin stitch.
3 Sew the eye edgings onto the eyes.
4 Tuck the loose yarn ends into the eyes, and add a tiny bit of stuffing if you want.
5 Sew the eyes onto the hat.
6 Sew the beak onto the hat.
7 Sew the button onto the hat.
8 Weave in ends.

LEFT MITTEN

Cuff

Using US 0 (2mm) double-pointed needles and A, cast on 22 (24, 26) sts and divide evenly among 3 needles. Join to work in the round, being careful not to twist. Place a marker at the beginning of the round.
Rounds 1-10 (1-12, 1-14): Work in k1, p1 rib.

Thumb gusset

Switch to US 3 (3.25mm) double-pointed needles to work rest of mitten.
Round 1: M1R, knit to end of round. 23 (25, 27) sts.
Round 2: Knit.
Round 3: M1R, k1, M1L, knit to end of round. 25 (27, 29) sts.
Round 4: Knit.
Round 5: M1R, k3, M1L, knit to end of round. 27 (29, 31) sts.
Round 6: Knit.
Round 7: M1R, k5, M1L, knit to end of round. 29 (31, 33) sts.
Round 8: Knit.
Round (9, 9) (two larger sizes only): M1R, k7, M1L, knit to end of round. (33, 35) sts.
Round 9 (10, 10): K1, place 7 (9, 9) thumb stitches on waste yarn and rejoin to work hand stitches in the round, k21 (23, 25). 22 (24, 26) sts.
Rounds 11-12 (two larger sizes only): Knit.
Round 10 (13, 13): K1 (2, 2), yo, k1, yo, k7 (7, 7), yo, k1, yo, k12 (13, 15). 26 (28, 30) sts.
Round 11 (14, 14): K2 (3, 3), yo, k1, yo, k9 (9, 9), yo, k1, yo, k13 (14, 16). 30 (32, 34) sts.
Round 12 (15, 15): K3 (4, 4), yo, k1, yo, k11 (11, 11), yo, k1, yo, k14 (15, 17). 34 (36, 38) sts.
Round 13 (16, 16): K4 (5, 5), yo, k1, yo, k13 (13, 13), yo, k1, yo, k15 (16, 18). 38 (40, 42) sts.
Close ears (see page 139 for diagrams)
Round 14 (17, 17): K1 (2, 2), sl next 4 sts, fold right-hand and left-hand needles parallel to each other with wrong sides together and points facing to the right (right needle is at the back), slip next st onto a crochet hook; it will be the 6th (7th, 7th) st in row.
Insert crochet hook into 5th (6th, 6th) st (from the right needle) and pull this through the loop on the hook. Continue in this way:
pull next st from the left needle through st on hook, pull next st from the right needle through st on hook,
Rep. from ** to ** until the last slipped st on the right needle has been pulled through the next st on the left needle, pull next st from the left needle through st on hook, slip this st back onto the left needle, unfold needles and hold normally, k7 (7, 7), sl next 4 sts.
Repeat the same way as the first ear until the last slipped st on the right needle has been pulled through the next st on the left needle, pull next st from the left needle through st on hook, slip this st back onto the left needle, k12 (13, 15). 22 (24, 26) sts.
Round 15-22 (18-26, 18-28): Knit.
Closing up the top
Round 23 (27, 29): K2tog to end of round. 11 (12, 13) sts.

Sew the beak in the center of the hat, with the eyes either side.

Round 24 (28, 30): Knit.
Round 25 (29, 31): K2tog to end of round. (If you get to the end of the round with only one stitch left, knit it.) 6 (6, 7) sts.
Cut a tail long enough to weave in. Pull it through all the stitches and remove them from the needles. Pull the tail tightly and secure. Weave in ends.

Thumb

Place 7 (9, 9) stitches from waste yarn onto US 3 (3.25mm) double-pointed needles. Rejoin yarn and pick up one extra stitch in the corner where the mitten meets the gusset. 8 (10, 10) sts.
Rounds 1-6 (1-6, 1-8): Knit.
Round 7 (7, 9): K2tog to end of round. 4 (5, 5) sts.
Finish off as for mitten Closing up the top.

RIGHT MITTEN

Cuff

Using US 0 (2mm) double-pointed needles and A, cast on 22 (24, 26) sts and divide evenly among 3 needles. Join to work in the round, being careful not to twist. Place a marker at the beginning of the round.
Rounds 1-10 (1-12, 1-14): Work in k1, p1 rib.

Thumb gusset

Switch to US 3 (3.25mm) double-pointed needles to work rest of mitten.
Round 1: M1R, knit to end of round. 23 (25, 27) sts.
Round 2: Knit.
Round 3: M1R, k1, M1L, knit to end of round. 25 (27, 29) sts.
Round 4: Knit.
Round 5: M1R, k3, M1L, knit to end of round. 27 (29, 31) sts.
Round 6: Knit.
Round 7: M1R, k5, M1L, knit to end of round. 29 (31, 33) sts.
Round 8: Knit.
Round (9, 9) (two larger sizes only): M1R, k7, M1L, knit to end of round. (33, 35) sts.
Round 9 (10, 10): K1, place 7 (9, 9) thumb stitches on waste yarn and rejoin to work hand stitches in the round, k21 (23, 25). 22 (24, 26) sts.
Rounds 11–12 (two larger sizes only): Knit.
Round 10 (13, 13): K12 (13, 15), yo, k1, yo, k7 (7, 7), yo, k1, yo, k1 (2, 2). 26 (28, 30) sts.
Round 11 (14, 14): K13 (14, 16), yo, k1, yo, k9 (9, 9), yo, k1, yo, k2 (3, 3). 30 (32, 34) sts.
Round 12 (15, 15): K14 (15, 17), yo, k1, yo, k11 (11, 11), yo, k1, yo, k3 (4, 4). 34 (36, 38) sts.

The eyes should fit perfectly on the top of the mittens.

Round 13 (16, 16): K15 (16, 18), yo, k1, yo, k13 (13, 13), yo, k1, yo, k4 (5, 5). 38 (40, 42) sts.
Close ears
Round 14 (17, 17): K12 (13, 15), sl next 4 sts, fold right-hand and left-hand needles parallel to each other with wrong sides together and points facing to the right (right needle is at the back), slip next st onto a crochet hook; it will be the 17th (18th, 20th) st in row.
Insert crochet hook into 16th (17th, 19th) st (from the right needle) and pull this through the loop on the hook. Continue in this way:
**pull next st from the left needle through st on hook,
pull next st from the right needle through st on hook,**
Rep. from ** to ** until the last slipped st on the right needle has been pulled through the next st on the left needle, pull next st from the left needle through st on hook, slip this st back onto the left needle, unfold needles and hold normally, k7 (7, 7), sl next 4 sts.
Repeat the same way as the first ear until the last slipped st on the right needle has been pulled through the next st on the left needle, pull next st from the left needle through st on hook, slip this st back onto the left needle, k1 (2, 2). 22 (24, 26) sts.
Round 15–22 (18–26, 18–28): Knit.
Closing up the top
Round 23 (27, 29): K2tog to end of round. 11 (12, 13) sts.
Round 24 (28, 30): Knit.
Round 25 (29, 31): K2tog to end of round. (If you get to the end of the round with only one stitch left, knit it.) 6 (6, 7) sts.
Finish as for left mitten Closing up the top.

Thumb

Place 7 (9, 9) stitches from waste yarn onto US 3 (3.25mm) double-pointed needles.

Rejoin yarn and pick up one extra stitch in the corner where the mitten meets the gusset. 8 (10, 10) sts.
Rounds 1-6 (1-6, 1-8): Knit.
Round 7 (7, 9): K2tog to end of round. 4 (5, 5) sts.
Finish as for left mitten Closing up the top.

Eyes (make 2)

With the crochet hook and B: Ch4. Join with sl st to form ring.
Round 1: Ch1, 9hdc through ring. 10hdc.
End with sl st to join. Fasten off, leaving a tail long enough for sewing.

Eye edging (make 2)

With the crochet hook and D: Ch4. Join with sl st to form ring.
Round 1: Ch2, 13dc through ring. 14dc.
End with sl st in next st to join. Fasten off, leaving a tail long enough for sewing.

Pupils (make 2)

With the crochet hook and C: Ch4. Join with sl st to form ring.
Round 1: 7sc through ring.
End with sl st in next st to join.
Fasten off, leaving a tail long enough for sewing.

Beak

With the crochet hook and E: Ch5.
Sl st in 2nd ch from hook, sc in 3rd ch from hook, hdc in 4th ch from hook. Fasten off.

FINISHING

1 Sew the pupils onto the eyes.
2 With B embroider two small highlights on pupils in satin stitch.
3 Sew the eyes onto the edgings of the eyes.
4 Sew the eyes onto the mittens.
5 Sew the beak onto the mittens.
6 Weave in ends.

Attach the leaves as shown here, and wise owl will have a tree to play in.

SCARF

With pair of US 3 (3.25mm) needles and D cast on 20 sts.
Rows 1-140: K1, p1 rib.
Bind off. Weave in ends.

Leaves (make 10)

Large leaves
(make 1 each in G and F)
Cast on 8 sts, leaving an 8in./20cm tail for sewing the leaf in place.
Row 1: Knit.
Row 2: K1, M1, k6, M1, k1. 10 sts.
Row 3: Knit.
Row 4: K1, M1, k8, M1, k1. 12 sts.
Rows 5-15: Garter st.
Row 16: K1, k2tog, k6, k2tog, k1. 10 sts.
Rows 17-20: Garter st.
Row 21: K1, k2tog, k4, k2tog, k1. 8 sts.
Rows 22-25: Garter st.
Row 26: K1, k2tog, k2, k2tog, k1. 6 sts.
Rows 27-28: Garter st.
Row 29: K1, *k2tog* twice, k1. 4 sts.
Row 30: Knit.
Cut a tail long enough to weave in. Pull it through all 4 stitches and remove them from the needles. Pull the tail tightly and secure.

Medium leaves
(make 1 each in I and H)
Cast on 4 sts, leaving an 8in./20cm tail for sewing the leaf in place.
Row 1: Knit.
Row 2: K1, M1, k2, M1, k1. 6 sts.
Row 3: Knit.
Row 4: K1, M1, k4, M1, k1. 8 sts.
Row 5: Knit.
Row 6: K1, M1, k6, M1, k1. 10 sts.
Rows 7-9: Garter st.
Row 10: K1, k2tog, k4, k2tog, k1. 8 sts.
Rows 11-14: Garter st.
Row 15: K1, k2tog, k2, k2tog, k1. 6 sts.
Rows 16-20: Garter st.
Row 21: K2, k2tog, k2. 5 sts.
Rows 22-24: Garter st.
Row 25: K2tog, k1, k2tog. 3 sts.
Row 26: Knit.
Cut a tail long enough to weave in. Pull it through all 3 stitches and remove them from the needles. Pull the tail tightly and secure.

Small leaves
(make 1 each in F, G, H, and I)
Cast on 4 sts, leaving an 8in./20cm tail for sewing the leaf in place.
Row 1: Knit.
Row 2: K1, M1, k2, M1, k1. 6 sts.
Row 3: Knit.
Row 4: K1, M1, k4, M1, k1. 8 sts.
Rows 5-10: Garter st.
Row 11: K1, k2tog, k2, k2tog, k1. 6 sts.

Rows 12-15: Garter st.
Row 16: K1, *k2tog* twice, k1. 4 sts.
Rows 17-20: Garter st.
Row 21: K1, k2tog, k1. 3 sts.
Row 22: Knit.
Finish off as for the 2 medium leaves.

Very small leaves
(make 2 in G)
Cast on 3 sts, leaving an 8in./20cm tail for sewing the leaf in place.
Row 1: Knit.
Row 2: K1, M1, k1, M1, k1. 5 sts.
Row 3: Knit.
Row 4: K1, M1, k3, M1, k1. 7 sts.
Row 5-7: Garter st.
Row 8: K1, k2tog, k1, k2tog, k1. 5 sts.
Row 9: Knit.
Row 10: K2tog, k1, k2tog. 3 sts.
Row 11: Knit.
Finish off as for the 2 medium leaves.

FINISHING
1 Sew the leaves onto the scarf.
2 Weave in ends.

huggable horrors

little monster

The mini-horns, eyes, and nails on this cute hat, mittens, and booties set will delight your little monster! The pattern is knitted except for some crochet spirals.

COVERALL HAT, MITTENS, AND BOOTIES
LEVEL: intermediate
SIZES
6-12 months (12-24 months, 2-3 years)
Finished measurements
From "cheek to cheek" around the hat:
14 (14½, 15)in. (36 [37, 38]cm)
Mitten circumference: 5½ (6, 6½)in. (13.75 [15, 16.25]cm)
Mitten length: 5½ (6½, 7)in. (14 [16.5, 18]cm)
Bootie circumference: 5½ (6½)in. (13.75 [15, 16.25] cm)
Booties heel to toe: 3 (3½, 4)in. (7.5 [9, 11]cm)
MATERIALS
HAT
Main yarn:
Color A: 1 x 3oz (85g) ball (135yd/123m) Lion Brand Jiffy Yarn, 100% acrylic, Violet
Small amounts:
Color B: Lion Brand Jiffy Yarn, 100% acrylic, Blossom
Color C: Lion Brand Jiffy Yarn, 100% acrylic, Fisherman
Color D: Lion Brand Jiffy Yarn, 100% acrylic, Black
Color E: Lion Brand Baby's First Yarn, 100% acrylic, Honey Bee
Needles:
• 1 pair of US 3 (3.25mm) needles
• US 3 (3.25mm) circular needle
• Stitch marker
• 4 x US 3 (3.25mm) double-pointed needles
• US C-2 (2.75mm) crochet hook

• Yarn needle
• Small amount of toy stuffing
MITTENS
Main yarn:
Color A: 1 x 3oz (85g) ball (135yd/123m) Lion Brand Jiffy Yarn, 100% acrylic, Violet
Small amounts:
Color B: Lion Brand Jiffy Yarn, 100% acrylic, Blossom
Color D: Lion Brand Jiffy Yarn, 100% acrylic, Black
Needles:
• 4 x US 0 (2mm) double-pointed needles
• 4 x US 3 (3.25mm) double-pointed needles
• US C-2 (2.75mm) crochet hook
• Yarn needle
BOOTIES
Main yarn:
Color A: 1 x 3oz (85g) ball (135yd/123m) Lion Brand Jiffy Yarn, 100% acrylic, Violet
Small amount:
Color E: Lion Brand Baby's First Yarn, 100% acrylic, Honey Bee
Needles:
• 4 x US 3 (3.25mm) double-pointed needles
• US C-2 (2.75mm) crochet hook
• Yarn needle
GAUGE
16 sts and 25 rows = 4in./10cm square in stockinette stitch, worked with US 3 (3.25mm) needles.
19 sts and 28 rows = 4in./10cm square in k1, p1 rib, worked with US 3 (3.25mm) needles.

HAT

Using a pair of US 3 (3.25mm) needles and A, cast on 57 (61, 65) sts.
Rows 1-6 (6, 6): K1, p1 rib.
Rows 7- 30 (30, 32): Work in stockinette stitch, starting with a k row.
Row 31 (31, 33): K18 (19, 21), k2tog, k17 (19, 19), k2tog, turn. 55 (59, 63) sts.
Row 32 (32, 34): Sl, p17 (19, 19), p2tog, turn. 54 (58, 62) sts.
Row 33 (33, 35): Sl, k17 (19, 19), k2tog, turn. 53 (57, 61) sts.
Rep. rows 32 (32, 34) and 33 (33, 35) to row 54 (56, 62). 32 (34, 34) sts.
Row 55 (57, 63): Sl, *p1, k1* rep. from * to * 8 (9, 9) times, p1, k2tog, turn. 31 (33, 33) sts.
Row 56 (58, 64): Sl, *k1, p1* rep. from * to * 8 (9, 9) times, k1, p2tog, turn. 30 (32, 32) sts.
Rep. rows 55 (57, 63) and 56 (58, 64) to row 66 (68, 74). 20 (22, 22) sts.

Neck ruff

Switch to a US 3 (3.25mm) circular needle. Place a marker at the beginning of the round.
Round 67 (69, 75): Sl, *p1, k1* rep. from * to * 8 (9, 9) times, p1, k2tog, pick up 13 (12, 12) sts on one side of the hat, cast on 7 (7, 7) sts, join to work in the round, being careful not to twist, pick up 13 (12, 12) sts on the other side of the hat. 52 (52, 52) sts.
Rounds 68-77 (70-81, 76-89): K1, p1 rib.
Round 78 (82, 90): K2 (3, 3), yo, k2, yo, k11 (11, 11), yo, k2, yo, k11 (11, 11), yo, k2, yo, k11 (11, 11), yo, k2, yo, k9 (8, 8). 60 (60, 60) sts.
Round 79 (83, 91): K3 (4, 4), yo, k2, yo, k13 (13, 13), yo, k2, yo, k13 (13, 13), yo, k2, yo, k13 (13, 13), yo, k2, yo, k10 (9, 9). 68 (68, 68) sts.
Round 80 (84, 92): K4 (5, 5), yo, k2, yo, k15 (15, 15), yo, k2, yo, k15 (15, 15), yo, k2, yo, k15 (15, 15), yo, k2, yo, k11 (10, 10). 76 (76, 76) sts.
Round 81 (85, 93): K5 (6, 6), yo, k2, yo, k17 (17, 17), yo, k2, yo, k17 (17, 17), yo, k2, yo, k17 (17, 17), yo, k2, yo, k12 (11, 11). 84 (84, 84) sts.
Round 82 (86, 94): K6 (7, 7), yo, k2, yo, k19 (19, 19), yo, k2, yo, k19 (19, 19), yo, k2, yo, k19 (19, 19), yo, k2, yo, k13 (12, 12). 92 (92, 92) sts.
Round 83 (87, 95): K7 (8, 8), yo, k2, yo, k21 (21, 21), yo, k2, yo, k21 (21, 21), yo, k2, yo, k21 (21, 21), yo, k2, yo, k14 (13, 13). 100 (100, 100) sts.
Round (88, 96) (two larger sizes only): K (9, 9), yo, k2, yo, k (23, 23), yo, k2, yo, k (23, 23), yo, k2, yo, k (23, 23), yo, k2, yo, k (14, 14). (108, 108) sts.

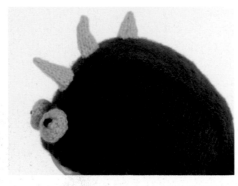

Sew the horns at even intervals across the top of the hat.

The little teeth poke out of the front of the hat.

Round (89, 97) (two larger sizes only): K (10, 10), yo, k2, yo, k (25, 25), yo, k2, yo, k (25, 25), yo, k2, yo, k (25, 25), yo, k2, yo, k (15, 15). (116, 116) sts.
Round (98) (largest size only): K (11), yo, k2, yo, k (27), yo, k2, yo, k (27), yo, k2, yo, k (27), yo, k2, yo, k (16). (124) sts.
Round (99) (largest size only): K (12), yo, k2, yo, k (29), yo, k2, yo, k (29), yo, k2, yo, k (29), yo, k2, yo, k (17). (132) sts.
Rounds 84-89 (90-95, 100-105) (all sizes): K1, p1 rib.
Bind off. Weave in ends.

Eyes (make 2)

This pattern is crocheted in spiral. Don't join at the end of a row but continue working.
With the crochet hook and B: Ch4. Join with sl st to form ring.
Round 1: 7sc through ring.
Round 2: 2sc in each sc. 14sc.
Round 3: 14sc.
Round 4: 14sc.
End with sl st in next st to join.
Fasten off, leaving a tail long enough for sewing.

Teeth (make 2)

With crochet hook and C:
Row 1: Ch6, 1hdc in 3rd ch from hook, 1hdc in 4th ch from hook, 1hdc in 5th ch from hook, 1hdc in 6th ch from hook.
Fasten off, leaving a tail long enough for sewing.

Horns (make 3)

2 big horns

Using 4 x US 3 (3.25mm) double-pointed needles and E, cast on 10 sts and divide evenly among 3 needles. Join to work in the round, being careful not to twist. Place a marker at the beginning of the round.
Rounds 1-2: Knit.
Round 3: *K1, k2tog* 3 times, k1. 7 sts.
Rounds 4-5: Knit.
Round 6: *K1, k2tog* twice, k1. 5 sts.
Rounds 7-8: Knit.
Round 9: K2tog, k1, k2tog. 3 sts.
Round 10: Knit.
Cut a tail long enough to weave in. Pull it through all 3 stitches and remove them from the needles. Pull the tail tightly and secure.

1 small horn

Using 4 x US 0 (2mm) double-pointed needles and E cast on 10 sts and divide evenly among 3 needles. Join to work in the round, being careful not to twist. Place a marker at the beginning of the round.
Round 1: Knit.
Round 2: *K1, k2tog* 3 times, k1. 7 sts.
Round 3: Knit.
Round 4: *K1, k2tog* twice, k1. 5 sts.
Rounds 5: Knit.
Round 6: K2tog, k1, k2tog. 3 sts.
Round 7: Knit.
Finish as for 2 big horns.

Each mitten has its very own little monster eye.

FINISHING

1 Using D, embroider 2 small pupils in satin stitch.
2 Tuck the loose yarn ends into the dome of the eyeball, and add a tiny bit of stuffing if you want.
3 Sew eyes onto the hat.
4 Sew the teeth onto the hat.
5 Tuck the loose yarn ends into the horns, and add a tiny bit of stuffing if you want.
6 Sew the horns onto the hat.
7 Weave in ends.

MITTENS

(MAKE 2)

Cuff

Using US 0 (2mm) double-pointed needles and A cast on 22 (24, 26) sts and divide evenly among 3 needles. Join to work in the round, being careful not to twist. Place a marker at the beginning of the round.
Rounds 1-10 (1-12, 1-14): Work in k1, p1 rib

Thumb gusset

Switch to US 3 (3.25mm) double-pointed needles to work rest of mitten.
Round 1: M1R, knit to end of round. 23 (25, 27) sts.
Round 2: Knit.
Round 3: M1R, k1, M1L, knit to end of round. 25 (27, 29) sts.
Round 4: Knit.
Round 5: M1R, k3, M1L, knit to end of round. 27 (29, 31) sts.
Round 6: Knit.
Round 7: M1R, k5, M1L, knit to end of round. 29 (31, 33) sts.
Round 8: Knit.
Round 9 (9, 9) (two larger sizes only): M1R, k7, M1L, knit to end of round. (33, 35) sts.
Round 9 (10, 10): K1, place 7 (9, 9) thumb stitches on waste yarn and rejoin to work hand stitches in the round, k21 (23, 25). 22 (24, 26) sts.
Rounds 10-22 (11-26, 11-28): Knit.
Closing up the top
Round 23 (27, 29): K2tog to end of round. 11 (12, 13) sts.
Round 24 (28, 30): Knit.
Round 25 (29, 31): K2tog to end of round. (If you get to the end of the round with only one stitch left, knit it.) 6 (6, 7) sts.
Cut a tail long enough to weave in. Pull it through all the stitches and remove them from the needles. Pull the tail tightly and secure. Weave in ends.

Thumb

Place 7 (9, 9) stitches from waste yarn onto US 3 (3.25mm) double-pointed needles. Rejoin yarn and pick up one extra stitch in the corner where the mitten meets the gusset. Place a marker at the beginning of the round. 8 (10, 10) sts.
Rounds 1-6 (1-6, 1-8): Knit.
Round 7 (7, 9): K2tog to end of round. 4 (5, 5) sts. Finish off as for mitten Closing up the top.

Eyes (make 2)

With the crochet hook and B: Ch4. Join with sl st to form ring.
Round 1: Ch2, 13dc. 14dc through ring. End with sl st in next st to join. Fasten off, leaving a tail long enough for sewing.

FINISHING

1 Embroider the pupils in satin stitch using D.
2 Sew eyes onto the mittens.
3 Weave in ends.

BOOTIES

(MAKE 2)

Using 4 x US 3 (3.25mm) double-pointed needles and A, cast on 24 (26, 28) sts and divide evenly among 3 needles. Join to work in the round, being careful not to twist. Place a marker at the beginning of the round.
Rounds 1-10 (1-12, 1-14): Work in k1, p1 rib.
Rounds 11-13 (13-15, 15-17): Knit.

Heel

Row 14 (16, 18): K12 (13, 14), turn.
Row 15 (17, 19): P12 (13, 14), turn.
Rep. rows 14 (16, 18) and 15 (17, 19) to row 19 (21, 23).
Row 20 (22, 24): K2, k2tog, k4 (5, 6), k2tog,

Even the booties have little claws!

turn. 22 (24, 26) sts.
Row 21 (23, 25): Sl, p4 (5, 6), p2tog, turn. 21 (23, 25) sts.
Row 22 (24, 26): Sl, k4 (5, 6), k2tog, turn. 20 (22, 24) sts.
Row 23 (25, 27): Sl, p4 (5, 6), p2tog, turn. 19 (21, 23) sts.
Work in rounds from now on.
Round 24 (26, 28): Sl, k4 (5, 6), k2tog, pick up 3 sts down side of heel, k12 (13, 14). 21 (23, 25) sts.
Round 25 (27, 29): Pick up 3 sts up side of heel, k21 (23, 25). 24 (26, 28) sts.
Rounds 26-40 (28-46, 30-52): Knit.
Closing up the toe
Round 41 (47, 53): K2tog to end of round. 12 (13, 14) sts.
Round 42 (48, 54): Knit.
Round 43 (49, 55): (If you are decreasing and get to the end of the round with only one stitch left, just knit it.) K2tog to end of round. 6 (7, 7) sts. Finish as for mitten Closing up the top.

Claws (make 6)

With the crochet hook and E: Ch5.
Sl st in 2nd ch from hook, sc in 3rd ch from hook, hdc in 4th ch from hook. Fasten off leaving a tail long enough for sewing.

FINISHING

1 Sew the nails onto the booties.
2 Weave in ends.

alien elf

The extraordinary ears and cable-patterned top of the hat make the alien elf truly original. The three-digit mittens will make your little one look out of this world!

COVERALL HAT AND MITTENS
LEVEL: advanced
SIZES
6-12 months (12-24 months, 2-3 years)
Finished measurements
From "cheek to cheek" around the hat:
14 (14½, 15)in. (36 [37, 38]cm)
Mitten circumference: 5½ (6, 6½)in.
(13.75 [15, 16.25]cm)
Mitten length: 5½ (6½, 7)in.
(14 [16.5, 18]cm)
MATERIALS
HAT
Yarn:
Color A: 1 x 3oz (85g) ball (135yd/123m)
Lion Brand Jiffy Yarn, 100% acrylic, Apple
Green
Color B: 1 x 3oz (85g) ball (135yd/123m)
Lion Brand Jiffy Yarn, 100% acrylic, Oat
Needles:
• 1 pair of US 3 (3.25mm) needles
• US 3 (3.25mm) circular needles
• Stitch marker
• Cable needle
• Yarn needle
MITTENS
Main yarn:
Color A: 1 x 3oz (85g) ball (135yd/123m)
Lion Brand Jiffy Yarn, 100% acrylic, Apple
Green
Small amount:
Color B: Lion Brand Jiffy Yarn, 100%
acrylic, Oat
Needles:
• 4 x US 0 (2mm) double-pointed needles
• 4 x US 3 (3.25mm) double-pointed
needles
• Yarn needle
GAUGE
16 sts and 25 rows = 4in./10cm square
in stockinette stitch, worked with US 3
(3.25mm) needles.
19 sts and 28 rows = 4in./10cm square
in k1, p1 rib, worked with US 3 (3.25mm)
needles.

HAT

Using a pair of US 3 (3.25mm) needles and A, cast on 57 (61, 65) sts.

Rows 1-6 (6, 6): K1, p1 rib.

Row 7 (7, 7): Knit.

Row 8 (8, 8): Purl.

Row 9 (9, 9): K24 (26, 28), sl next 2 sts to cn and hold in back, k2, k2 from cn, k1, sl next 2 sts to cn and hold in front, k2, k2 from cn, k24 (26, 28).

Row 10 (10, 10): Purl.

Row 11 (11, 11): K22 (24, 26), sl next 2 sts to cn and hold in back, k2, k2 from cn, k5, sl next 2 sts to cn and hold in front, k2, k2 from cn, k22 (24, 26).

Row 12 (12, 12): Purl.

Row 13 (13, 13): K20 (22, 24), sl next 2 sts to cn and hold in back, k2, k2 from cn, k9, sl next 2 sts to cn and hold in front, k2, k2 from cn, k20 (22, 24).

Row 14 (14, 14): Purl.

Row 15 (15, 15): K18 (20, 22), sl next 2 sts to cn and hold in back, k2, k2 from cn, k13, sl next 2 sts to cn and hold in front, k2, k2 from cn, k18 (20, 22).

A 2 by 2 cable-knit pattern is used to create the design on the front of the hat.

Row 16 (16, 16): Purl.
Row 17 (17, 17): K24 (26, 28), sl next 2 sts to cn and hold in back, k2, k2 from cn, k1, sl next 2 sts to cn and hold in front, k2, k2 from cn, k24 (26, 28).
Row 18 (18, 18): Purl.
Row 19 (19, 19): K22 (24, 26), sl next 2 sts to cn and hold in back, k2, k2 from cn, k5, sl next 2 sts to cn and hold in front, k2, k2 from cn, k22 (24, 26).
Row 20 (20, 20): Purl.
Row 21 (21, 21): K20 (22, 24), sl next 2 sts to cn and hold in back, k2, k2 from cn, k9, sl next 2 sts to cn and hold in front, k2, k2 from cn, k20 (22, 24).

Row 22 (22, 22): Purl.
Row 23 (23, 23): K18 (20, 22), sl next 2 sts to cn and hold in back, k2, k2 from cn, k13, sl next 2 sts to cn and hold in front, k2, k2 from cn, k18 (20, 22).
Row 24 (24, 24): Purl.
Row 25 (25, 25): K24 (26, 28), sl next 2 sts to cn and hold in back, k2, k2 from cn, k1, sl next 2 sts to cn and hold in front, k2, k2 from cn, k24 (26, 28).
Row 26 (26, 26): Purl.
Row 27 (27, 27): K22 (24, 26), sl next 2 sts to cn and hold in back, k2, k2 from cn, k5, sl next 2 sts to cn and hold in front, k2, k2 from cn, k22 (24, 26).

Sew the ears on in the middle of the side of the hat.

Row 28 (28, 28): Purl.

Row 29 (29, 29): K20 (22, 24), sl next 2 sts to cn and hold in back, k2, k2 from cn, k9, sl next 2 sts to cn and hold in front, k2, k2 from cn, k20 (22, 24).

Row 30 (30, 30): Purl.

Row (31) (the largest size only): Knit.

Row (32) (the largest size only): Purl.

Row 31 (31, 33): K18 (19, 21), k2tog, k17 (19, 19), k2tog, turn. 55 (59, 63) sts.

Row 32 (32, 34): Sl, p17 (19, 19), p2tog, turn. 54 (58, 62) sts.

Row 33 (33, 35): Sl, k17 (19, 19), k2tog, turn. 53 (57, 61) sts.

Rep. rows 32 (32, 34) and 33 (33, 35) to row 54 (56, 62). 32 (34, 34) sts.

Row 55 (57, 63): Sl, *p1, k1* rep. from * to * 8 (9, 9) times, p1, k2tog, turn. 31 (33, 33) sts.

Row 56 (58, 64): Sl, *k1, p1* rep. from * to * 8 (9, 9) times, k1, p2tog, turn. 30 (32, 32) sts.

Rep. rows 55 (57, 63) and 56 (58, 64) to row 66 (68, 74). 20 (22, 22) sts.

Neck ruff

Switch to US 3 (3.25mm) circular needles and B. Place a marker at the beginning of the round.

Round 67 (69, 75): Sl, *p1, k1* rep. from * to * 8 (9, 9) times, p1, k2tog, pick up 13 (12, 12) sts on one side of the hat, cast on 7 (7, 7) sts, join to work in the round, being careful not to twist, pick up 13 (12, 12) sts on the other side of the hat. 52 (52, 52) sts.

Rounds 68-77 (70-81, 76-89): K1, p1 rib.

Round 78 (82, 90): K2 (3, 3), yo, k2, yo, k11 (11, 11), yo, k2, yo, k11 (11, 11), yo, k2, yo, k11 (11, 11), yo, k2, yo, k9 (8, 8). 60 (60, 60) sts.

Round 79 (83, 91): K3 (4, 4), yo, k2, yo, k13 (13, 13), yo, k2, yo, k13 (13, 13), yo, k2, yo, k13 (13, 13), yo, k2, yo, k10 (9, 9). 68 (68, 68) sts.

Round 80 (84, 92): K4 (5, 5), yo, k2, yo, k15 (15, 15), yo, k2, yo, k15 (15, 15), yo, k2, yo, k15 (15, 15), yo, k2, yo, k11 (10, 10). 76 (76, 76) sts.

Round 81 (85, 93): K5 (6, 6), yo, k2, yo, k17 (17, 17), yo, k2, yo, k17 (17, 17), yo, k2, yo, k17 (17, 17), yo, k2, yo, k12 (11, 11). 84 (84, 84) sts.

Round 82 (86, 94): K6 (7, 7), yo, k2, yo, k19 (19, 19), yo, k2, yo, k19 (19, 19), yo, k2, yo, k19 (19, 19), yo, k2, yo, k13 (12, 12). 92 (92, 92) sts.

Round 83 (87, 95): K7 (8, 8), yo, k2, yo, k21 (21, 21), yo, k2, yo, k21 (21, 21), yo, k2, yo, k21 (21, 21), yo, k2, yo, k14 (13, 13). 100 (100, 100) sts.

Round (88, 96) (two larger sizes only): K (9, 9), yo, k2, yo, k (23, 23), yo, k2, yo, k (23, 23), yo, k2, yo, k (23, 23), yo, k2, yo, k (14, 14). (108, 108) sts.

Round (89, 97) (two larger sizes only): K (10, 10), yo, k2, yo, k (25, 25), yo, k2, yo, k (25, 25), yo, k2, yo, k (25, 25), yo, k2, yo, k (15, 15). (116, 116) sts.

The contrasting color of the neck ruff looks great from the back.

Round (98) (largest size only): K (11), yo, k2, yo, k (27), yo, k2, yo, k (27), yo, k2, yo, k (27), yo, k2, yo, k (16). (124) sts.

Round (99) (largest size only): K (12), yo, k2, yo, k (29), yo, k2, yo, k (29), yo, k2, yo, k (29), yo, k2, yo, k (17). (132) sts.

Rounds 84-89 (90-95, 100-105) (all sizes): K1, p1 rib.
Bind off. Weave in ends.

Ears (make 2)

Using a pair of US 3 (3.25mm) needles and A, cast on 25 sts.
Round 1: Knit.
Round 2: Knit.
Round 3: K1, k2tog, k19, k2tog, k1. 23 sts.
Round 4: Knit.
Round 5: K1, k2tog, k17, k2tog, k1. 21 sts.
Round 6: Knit.
Round 7: K1, k2tog, k15, k2tog, k1. 19 sts.
Round 8: Knit.
Round 9: K1, k2tog, k13, k2tog, k1. 17 sts.
Round 10: Knit.
Round 11: K1, k2tog, k11, k2tog, k1. 15 sts.
Round 12: Knit.

The garter-stitch ears attached to a stockinette-stitch hat give this hat a unique look.

Round 13: K1, k2tog, k9, k2tog, k1. 13 sts.
Round 14: Knit.
Round 15: K1, k2tog, k7, k2tog, k1. 11 sts.
Round 16: Knit.
Round 17: K1, k2tog, k5, k2tog, k1. 9 sts.
Round 18: Knit.
Round 19: K1, k2tog, k3, k2tog, k1. 7 sts.
Rounds 20-22: Knit.
Round 23: K1, k2tog, k1, k2tog, k1. 5 sts.
Round 24: Knit.
Round 25: K1, k2tog, k k2. 4 sts.
Round 26: Knit.
Round 27: K1, k2tog, k1. 3 sts.
Round 28: Knit.
Cut tail long enough to weave in. Pull through all 3 stitches. Remove them from needle. Pull the tail tightly and secure. Make a strong knot. Weave in end.

FINISHING

1 Fold both ears into three equal sections (like folding a letter into an envelope) to mirror each other.
2 Sew the ears to the hat in the position shown.
3 Weave in ends.

MITTENS

(MAKE 2)

Cuff

Using US 0 (2mm) double-pointed needles and B, cast on 22 (24, 26) sts and divide evenly among 3 needles. Join to work in the round, being careful not to twist. Place a marker at the beginning of the round.
Rounds 1-10 (1-12, 1-14): K1, p1 rib.

Thumb gusset

Switch to US 3 (3.25mm) double-pointed needles to work rest of mitten.
Round 1: M1R, knit to end of round. 23 (25, 27) sts.
Round 2: Knit.
Round 3: M1R, k1, M1L, knit to end of round. 25 (27, 29) sts.
Round 4: Knit.
Round 5: M1R, k3, M1L, knit to end of round. 27 (29, 31) sts.
Round 6: Knit.
Round 7: M1R, k5, M1L, knit to end of round. 29 (31, 33) sts.
Round 8: Knit.
Round (9, 9) (two larger sizes only): M1R, k7, M1L, knit to end of round. (33, 35) sts.
Round 9 (10, 10): K1, place 7 (9, 9) thumb stitches on waste yarn and rejoin to work hand stitches in the round, k21 (23, 25). 22 (24, 26) sts.
Rounds 10-13 (11-15, 11-16): Knit.

Index and middle fingers

Round 14 (16, 17): K6 (6, 7), place next 11 (12, 13) sts on waste yarn, cast on 2 sts, k5 (6, 6). 13 (14, 15) sts.

Rounds 15-22 (17-26, 18-28): Knit.

Round 23 (27, 29): K2tog to end of round. (If you get to the end of the round with only one stitch left, just knit it). 7 (7, 8) sts.

Round 24 (28, 30): Knit.

Cut a tail long enough to weave in. Pull it through all the stitches and remove them from the needles. Pull the tail tightly and secure.

Ring and pinky fingers

Place 11 (12, 13) stitches from waste yarn onto US 3 (3.25mm) double-pointed needles. Rejoin yarn and pick up 2 sts from 2 cast-on sts. Place a marker at the beginning of the round. 13 (14, 15) sts.

Round 14-22 (16-26, 17-28): Knit.

Round 23 (27, 29): K2tog to end of round. (If you get to the end of the round with only one stitch left, just knit it). 7 (7, 8) sts.

Round 24 (28, 30): Knit.

Finish as for the Index and middle fingers.

Thumb

Place 7 (9, 9) stitches from waste yarn onto US 3 (3.25mm) double-pointed needles. Rejoin yarn. Pick up one extra stitch in the corner where the mitten meets the gusset. 8 (10, 10) sts.

Rounds 1-6 (1-6, 1-8): Knit.

Round 7 (7, 9): K2tog to end of round. 4 (5, 5) sts. Finish as for the Index and middle fingers.

Little ones will love playing in these alien mittens with two chunky fingers!

miniature robot

This playful hat sports a fantastic antenna with a red light bulb—as do the mittens. Classic soft booties complete the set. Some crocheting in spirals is required.

COVERALL HAT, MITTENS, AND BOOTIES

LEVEL: advanced

SIZES
6-12 months (12-24 months, 2-3 years)

Finished measurements

From "cheek to cheek" around the hat:
14 (14½, 15)in. (36 [37, 38]cm)

Mitten circumference: 5½ (6, 6½)in. (13.75 [15, 16.25]cm)

Mitten length: 5½ (6½, 7)in. (14 [16.5, 18]cm)

Booties heel to toe:
3 (3½, 4)in. (7.5 [9, 11]cm)

MATERIALS

HAT
Main yarn:
Color A: 1 x 3oz (85g) ball (135yd/123m) Lion Brand Jiffy Yarn, 100% acrylic, Silver Heather

Small amounts:
Color B: Lion Brand Jiffy Yarn, 100% acrylic, White
Color C: Lion Brand Jiffy Yarn, 100% acrylic, True Red
Color D: Lion Brand Jiffy Yarn, 100% acrylic, Black

Needles:
- 1 pair of US 3 (3.25mm) needles
- US 3 (3.25mm) circular needle
- Stitch marker
- 4 x US 3 (3.25mm) double-pointed needles
- US C-2 (2.75mm) crochet hook
- Yarn needle
- Small amount of toy stuffing

MITTENS
Main yarn:
Color A: 1 x 3oz (85g) ball (135yd/123m) Lion Brand Jiffy Yarn, 100% acrylic, Silver Heather

Small amounts:
Color B: Lion Brand Jiffy Yarn, 100% acrylic, White
Color C: Lion Brand Jiffy Yarn, 100% acrylic, True Red
Color D: Lion Brand Jiffy Yarn, 100% acrylic, Black

Needles:
- 4 x US 0 (2mm) double-pointed needles
- 4 x US 3 (3.25mm) double-pointed needles
- US C-2 (2.75mm) crochet hook
- Yarn needle

BOOTIES
Main yarn:
Color A: Lion Brand Jiffy Yarn, 100% acrylic, Silver Heather (2.1oz [60g], 95yd [87m])

Small amounts:
Color B: Lion Brand Jiffy Yarn, 100% acrylic, White
Color C: Lion Brand Jiffy Yarn, 100% acrylic, True Red
Color D: Lion Brand Jiffy Yarn, 100% acrylic, Black

Needles:
- 4 x US 3 (3.25mm) double-pointed needles
- Yarn needle

GAUGE
16 sts and 25 rows = 4in./10cm square in stockinette stitch, worked with US 3 (3.25mm) needles.

19 sts and 28 rows = 4in./10cm square in k1, p1 rib, worked with US 3 (3.25mm) needles.

HAT
Using a pair of US 3 (3.25mm) needles and A, cast on 57 (61, 65) sts.

Rows 1-6 (6, 6): K1, p1 rib.

Rows 7-30 (30, 32): Work in stockinette stitch, starting with a k row.

Row 31 (31, 33): K18 (19, 21), k2tog, k17 (19, 19), k2tog, turn. 55 (59, 63) sts.

Row 32 (32, 34): Sl, p17 (19, 19), p2tog, turn. 54 (58, 62) sts.

Row 33 (33, 35): Sl, k17 (19, 19), k2tog, turn. 53 (57, 61) sts.

Rep. rows 32 (32, 34) and 33 (33, 35) to row 54 (56, 62). 32 (34, 34) sts.

Row 55 (57, 63): Sl, *p1, k1* rep. from * to * 8 (9, 9) times, p1, k2tog, turn. 31 (33, 33) sts.

Row 56 (58, 64): Sl, *k1, p1* rep. from * to * 8 (9, 9) times, k1, p2tog, turn. 30 (32, 32) sts.

Rep. rows 55 (57, 63) and 56 (58, 64) to row 66 (68, 74). 20 (22, 22) sts.

Neck ruff
Switch to a US 3 (3.25mm) circular needle. Place a marker at the beginning of the round.

Round 67 (69, 75): Sl, *p1, k1* rep. from * to * 8 (9, 9) times, p1, k2tog, pick up 13 (12, 12) sts on one side of the hat, cast on 7 (7, 7) sts, join to work in the round, being careful not to twist, pick up 13 (12, 12) sts on the other side of the hat. 52 (52, 52) sts.

Rounds 68-77 (70-81, 76-89): K1, p1 rib.

Round 78 (82, 90): K2 (3, 3), yo, k2, yo, k11 (11, 11), yo, k2, yo, k11 (11, 11), yo, k2, yo, k11 (11, 11), yo, k2, yo, k9 (8, 8). 60 (60, 60) sts.

Round 79 (83, 91): K3 (4, 4), yo, k2, yo, k13 (13, 13), yo, k2, yo, k13 (13, 13), yo, k2, yo, k13 (13, 13), yo, k2, yo, k10 (9, 9). 68 (68, 68) sts.

Round 80 (84, 92): K4 (5, 5), yo, k2, yo, k15 (15, 15), yo, k2, yo, k15 (15, 15), yo, k2, yo, k15 (15, 15), yo, k2, yo, k11 (10, 10). 76 (76, 76) sts.

Round 81 (85, 93): K5 (6, 6), yo, k2, yo, k17 (17, 17), yo, k2, yo, k17 (17, 17), yo, k2, yo, k17 (17, 17), yo, k2, yo, k12 (11, 11). 84 (84, 84) sts.

Round 82 (86, 94): K6 (7, 7), yo, k2, yo, k19 (19, 19), yo, k2, yo, k19 (19, 19), yo, k2, yo, k19 (19, 19), yo, k2, yo, k13 (12, 12). 92 (92, 92) sts.

Round 83 (87, 95): K7 (8, 8), yo, k2, yo, k21 (21, 21), yo, k2, yo, k21 (21, 21), yo, k2, yo, k21 (21, 21), yo, k2, yo, k14 (13, 13). 100 (100, 100) sts.

Round (88, 96) (two larger sizes only): K (9, 9), yo, k2, yo, k (23, 23), yo, k2, yo, k (23, 23), yo, k2, yo, k (23, 23), yo, k2, yo, k (14, 14). (108, 108) sts.

Round (89, 97) (two larger sizes only): K (10, 10), yo, k2, yo, k (25, 25), yo, k2, yo, k (25, 25), yo, k2, yo, k (25, 25), yo, k2, yo, k (15, 15). (116, 116) sts.
Round (98) (largest size only): K (11), yo, k2, yo, k (27), yo, k2, yo, k (27), yo, k2, yo, k (27), yo, k2, yo, k (16). (124) sts.
Round (99) (largest size only): K (12), yo, k2, yo, k (29), yo, k2, yo, k (29), yo, k2, yo, k (29), yo, k2, yo, k (17). (132) sts.
Rounds 84-89 (90-95, 100-105) (all sizes): K1, p1 rib.
Bind off. Weave in ends.

Eyes (make 2 in B), Ears (make 2 in C), Bottom part of antenna (make 1 in A)

This pattern is crocheted in spiral. Don't join at the end of a row but continue working. With the crochet hook, Ch4. Join with sl st to form ring.
Round 1: 7sc through ring.
Round 2: 2sc in each sc. 14sc.
Round 3: 14sc.
Round 4: 14sc.
End with sl st in next st to join.
Fasten off, leaving a tail long enough for sewing.

Edging of the ear (make 2)

Using 4 x US 3 (3.25mm) double-pointed needles and A, cast on 22 sts and divide evenly among 3 needles. Join to work in the round, being careful not to twist. Place a marker at the beginning of the round.
Rounds 1-2: K1, p1 rib.
Bind off, leaving a tail long enough for sewing.

Edging of the eyes

Using 4 x US 3 (3.25mm) double-pointed needles and A, cast on 40 sts and divide evenly among 3 needles. Join to work in the round, being careful not to twist. Place a marker at the beginning of the round.
Rounds 1-2: K1, p1 rib.
Bind off, leaving a tail long enough for sewing.

Middle part of antenna

Using 4 x US 3 (3.25mm) double-pointed needles and A, cast on 6 sts and divide evenly among 3 needles. Join to work in the round, being careful not to twist. Place a marker at the beginning of the round.
Rounds 1-15: Knit.
Cut a tail long enough to weave in. Pull through all 6 stitches and remove them from the needles. Pull the tail tightly and secure. Weave in ends.

Red bulb (top of antenna)

This pattern is crocheted in spiral. Don't join at the end of a row but continue working.

The mittens have a complete robot face with little antennae.

With the crochet hook and C: Ch3. Join with sl st to form ring.
Round 1: 6sc through ring.
Round 2: 2sc in each sc. 12sc.
Round 3: 12sc.
Round 4: 12sc, lightly stuff the bulb.
Round 5: (Sc into next st, skip next st) 6 times. 6sc.
End with sl st in next st to join. Fasten off.
Cut a tail and pull it through all 6 stitches. Pull the tail tightly and secure. Weave in ends.

FINISHING

1 Using D, embroider 2 small pupils on eyes.
2 Sew the edging of the eyes around the eyes.
3 Tuck the loose yarn ends into the dome of the eyeball, and add a tiny bit of stuffing if you want.
4 Sew the eyes onto the hat.
5 Sew the edging of the ears around the ears.
6 Tuck the loose yarn ends into the ears, and add a tiny bit of stuffing if you want.
7 Sew the ears onto the hat.
8 Lightly stuff the middle part of the antenna.
9 Sew the bulb onto the middle of the antenna. Sew the middle part of the antenna onto the bottom of the antenna. Sew the antenna onto the hat.
10 Weave in ends.

MITTENS

(MAKE 2)

Cuff

Using US 0 (2mm) double-pointed needles and A, cast on 22 (24, 26) sts and divide evenly among 3 needles. Join to work in the round, being careful not to twist. Place a marker at the beginning of the round.
Rounds 1-10 (1-12, 1-14): Work in k1, p1 rib.

Thumb gusset

Switch to US 3 (3.25mm) double-pointed needles to work rest of mitten.
Round 1: M1R, knit to end of round. 23 (25, 27) sts.
Round 2: Knit.
Round 3: M1R, k1, M1L, knit to end of round. 25 (27, 29) sts.
Round 4: Knit.
Round 5: M1R, k3, M1L, knit to end of round. 27 (29, 31) sts.
Round 6: Knit.
Round 7: M1R, k5, M1L, knit to end of round. 29 (31, 33) sts.
Round 8: Knit.
Round (9, 9) (two larger sizes only): M1R, k7, M1L, knit to end of round. (33, 35) sts.

Round 9 (10, 10): K1, place 7 (9, 9) thumb stitches on waste yarn and rejoin to work hand stitches in the round, k21 (23, 25). 22 (24, 26) sts.

Rounds 10-22 (11-26, 11-28): Knit.

Closing up the top

Round 23 (27, 29): K2tog to end of round. 11 (12, 13) sts.

Round 24 (28, 30): Knit.

Round 25 (29, 31): K2tog to end of round. (If you get to the end of the round with only one stitch left, knit it.) 6 (6, 7) sts.

Round 26 (30, 32): K2tog, k1, k2tog, k1. 4 (4, 5) sts.

Round (33) (largest size only): K2tog, k3. (4) sts.

Rounds 27-31 (31-35, 34-38): Knit.

Cut a tail long enough to weave in. Pull it through all the stitches and remove them from the needles. Pull the tail tightly and secure. Weave in ends.

Thumb

Place 7 (9, 9) stitches from waste yarn onto US 3 (3.25mm) double-pointed needles. Rejoin yarn and pick up one extra stitch in the corner where the mitten meets the gusset. 8 (10, 10) sts.

Rounds 1-6 (1-6, 1-8): Knit.

Round 7 (7, 9): K2tog to end of round. 4 (5, 5) sts.

Finish as for mitten Closing up the top.

Eyes and ears (make 4 in B, make 4 in C)

With the crochet hook, make 4 with B, make 4 with C: Ch4. Join with sl st to form ring.

Round 1: 7sc through ring.

End with sl st in next st to join.

Fasten off, leaving a tail long enough for sewing.

FINISHING

1 Using D, embroider 4 small pupils on eyes in satin stitch.

2 Sew the eyes onto the mittens.

3 Sew the ears onto the mittens.

4 With C, embroider the bulb on the antenna in satin stitch.

5 With D, embroider the mouth on mittens in backstitch.

6 Weave in ends.

BOOTIES

(MAKE 2)

Using 4 x US 3 (3.25mm) double-pointed needles and A, cast on 24 (26, 28) sts and divide evenly among 3 double-pointed needles. Join to work in the round, being careful not to twist. Place a marker at the beginning of the round.

Rounds 1-12 (1-12, 1-12): Knit.

Round 13 (13, 13): *Fold your hem with the right sides facing each other. Insert your right-hand needle through the first stitch of your cast-on row and place it on your left-hand needle. Knit the picked-up stitch and your first stitch together*, rep. from * to * 24 (26, 28) times (to end of round).

Rounds 14-16 (14-17, 14-18): Knit.

Heel

Row 17 (18, 19): K12 (13, 14), turn.

Row 18 (19, 20): P12 (13, 14), turn.

Rep. rows 17 (18, 19) and 18 (19, 20) to row 22 (23, 24).

Row 23 (24, 25): K2, k2tog, k4 (5, 6), k2tog, turn. 22 (24, 26) sts.

Row 24 (25, 26): Sl, p4 (5, 6), p2tog, turn. 21 (23, 25) sts.

Row 25 (26, 27): Sl, k4 (5, 6), k2tog, turn. 20 (22, 24) sts.

Row 26 (27, 28): Sl, p4 (5, 6), p2tog, turn. 19 (21, 23) sts.

Work in rounds from now on.

Round 27 (28, 29): Sl, k4 (5, 6), k2tog, pick up 3 sts down side of heel, k12 (13, 14). 21 (23, 25) sts.

Round 28 (29, 30): Pick up 3 sts up side of heel, k21 (23, 25). 24 (26, 28) sts.

Rounds 29-43 (30-48, 31-53): Knit.

Closing up the toe

Round 44 (49, 54): K2tog to end of round. 12 (13, 14) sts.

Round 45 (50, 55): Knit.

Round 46 (51, 56): (If you are decreasing and get to the end of the round with only one stitch left, just knit it.) K2tog to end of round. 6 (7, 7) sts.

Cut a tail long enough to weave in. Pull through all stitches and remove them from the needles. Pull the tail tightly and secure. Weave in ends.

Classic soft gray booties complete the robot outfit.

dinky dragon

Knitted all in one color, the spines down the back of the hat are mirrored on the little mittens. This project is a worthwhile challenge for experienced knitters.

COVERALL HAT AND MITTENS
LEVEL: advanced
SIZES
6-12 months (12-24 months, 2-3 years)
Finished measurements
From "cheek to cheek" around the hat:
14 (14½, 15)in. (36 [37, 38]cm)
Mitten circumference: 5½ (6, 6½)in.
(13.75 [15, 16.25]cm)
Mitten length: 5½ (6½, 7)in.
(14 [16.5, 18]cm)
Materials
HAT
Yarn:
1 x 3oz (85g) ball (135yd/123m) Lion Brand Jiffy Yarn, 100% acrylic, Avocado (3oz [85g], 135yd [123m])
Needles:
• 1 pair of US 3 (3.25mm) needles
• US 3 (3.25mm) circular needle
• US C-2 (2.75mm) crochet hook
• Stitch marker
• Yarn needle
MITTENS
1 x 3oz (85g) ball (135yd/123m) Lion Brand Jiffy Yarn, 100% acrylic, Avocado
Needles:
• 4 x US 0 (2mm) double-pointed needles
• 4 x US 3 (3.25mm) double-pointed needles
• US C-2 (2.75mm) crochet hook
• Stitch marker
• Yarn needle
GAUGE
16 sts and 25 rows = 4in./10cm square in stockinette stitch, worked with US 3 (3.25mm) needles.
19 sts and 28 rows = 4in./10cm square in k1, p1 rib, worked with US 3 (3.25mm) needles.

HAT

SIZE 6-12 MONTHS
Using a pair of US 3 (3.25mm) needles, cast on 57 sts.
Rows 1-6: K1, p1 rib.
Row 7: K28, yo, k1, yo, k28. 59 sts.
Row 8: P29, yo, p1, yo, p29. 61 sts.
Row 9: K30, yo, k1, yo, k30. 63 sts.
Row 10: P31, yo, p1, yo, p31. 65 sts.
Row 11: K32, yo, k1, yo, k32. 67 sts.
Row 12: P33, yo, p1, yo, p33. 69 sts.
Row 13: K34, yo, k1, yo, k34. 71 sts.
Row 14: P35, yo, p1, yo, p35. 73 sts.
Close first spine (see page 139 for diagrams)
Row 15: K28, sl next 8 sts, fold right hand and left hand needles parallel to each other with wrong sides facing and points facing to the right (right needle is at the back), slip next st onto a crochet hook; it will be the 37th st in row. Insert crochet hook into 36th st (from the right needle) and pull this through the loop on hook.
*Continue in this way:
**pull next st from the left needle through st on hook,
pull next st from right needle through st on hook. **
Rep. from ** to ** until the last slipped st on the right needle has been pulled through the next st on the left needle, pull next st from the left needle through st on hook, slip this st back onto the left needle, unfold needles and hold normally*, k29. 57 sts.
Row 16: Purl.
Row 17: K28, yo, k1, yo, k28. 59 sts.
Row 18: P29, yo, p1, yo, p28. 61 sts.
Row 19: K30, yo, k1, yo, k30. 63 sts.
Row 20: P31, yo, p1, yo, p31. 65 sts.
Row 21: K32, yo, k1, yo, k32. 67 sts.
Row 22: P33, yo, p1, yo, p33. 69 sts.
Row 23: K34, yo, k1, yo, k34. 71 sts.
Row 24: P35, yo, p1, yo, p35. 73 sts.
Rows 25-30: Rep. rows 15-20. 65 sts.
Row 31: K18, k2tog, k12, yo, k1, yo, k12, k2tog, turn. 65 sts.
Row 32: Sl, p13, yo, p1, yo, p13, p2tog, turn. 66 sts.
Row 33: Sl, k14, yo, k1, yo, k14, k2tog, turn. 67 sts.
Row 34: Sl, p15, yo, p1, yo, p15, p2tog, turn. 68 sts.
Close spine
Row 35: Sl, k8, sl next 8 sts, fold right-hand and left-hand needles parallel to each other with wrong sides facing and points facing to the right (right needle is at the back), slip next st onto a

The dragon spines are sewn right down the center of the hat.

crochet hook; it will be the 18th st in row.
Insert crochet hook into 17th st (from the right needle) and pull this through the loop on hook.
Rep. the same way from * to * as (row 15), k9, k2tog, turn. 51 sts.
Row 36: Sl, p17, p2tog, turn. 50 sts.
Row 37: Sl, k8, yo, k1, yo, k8, k2tog, turn. 51 sts.
Row 38: Sl, p9, yo, p1, yo, p9, p2tog, turn. 52 sts.
Row 39: Sl, k10, yo, k1, yo, k10, k2tog, turn. 53 sts.
Row 40: Sl, p11, yo, p1, yo, p11, p2tog, turn. 54 sts.
Row 41: Sl, k12, yo, k1, yo, k12, k2tog, turn. 55 sts.
Row 42: Sl, p13, yo, p1, yo, p13, p2tog, turn. 56 sts.
Row 43: Sl, k14, yo, k1, yo, k14, k2tog, turn. 57 sts.
Row 44: Sl, p15, yo, p1, yo, p15, p2tog, turn. 58 sts.
Close spine
Row 45: Work the same as row 35. 41 sts.
Rows 46-54: Rep. rows 36-44. 48 sts.
Close spine
Row 55: Sl, *p1, k1* 4 times, sl next 8 sts, fold right hand and left hand needles parallel to each other with wrong sides facing and points facing to the right (right needle is at the back), slip next st onto a crochet hook; it will be the 18th st in row.

Insert crochet hook into 17th st (from the right needle) and pull this through the loop on hook. Rep. the same way from * to * as Close first spine (row 15), k1, *k1, p1* 4 times, k2tog, turn. 31 sts.

Row 56: Sl, *k1, p1* 3 times, k1, p3, *k1, p1* 3 times, k1, p2tog. 30 sts.

Row 57: Sl, *p1, k1* 4 times, yo, k1, yo, *k1, p1* 4 times, k2tog, turn. 31 sts.

Row 58: Sl, *k1, p1* 3 times, k1, p2, yo, p1, yo, p2, *k1, p1* 3 times, k1, p2tog, turn. 32 sts.

Row 59: Sl, *p1, k1* 3 times, p1, k3, yo, k1, yo, k3, *p1, k1* 3 times, p1, k2tog, turn. 33 sts.

Row 60: Sl, *k1, p1* 3 times, k1, p4, yo, p1, yo, p4, *k1, p1* 3 times, k1, p2tog, turn. 34 sts.

Row 61: Sl, *p1, k1* 3 times, p1, k5, yo, k1, yo, k5, *p1, k1* 3 times, p1, k2tog, turn. 35 sts.

Row 62: Sl, *k1, p1* 3 times, k1, p6, yo, p1, yo, p6, *k1, p1* 3 times, k1, p2tog, turn. 36 sts.

Row 63: Sl, *p1, k1* 3 times, p1, k7, yo, k1, yo, k7, *p1, k1* 3 times, p1, k2tog, turn. 37 sts.

Row 64: Sl, *k1, p1* 3 times, k1, p8, yo, p1, yo, p8, *k1, p1* 3 times, k1, p2tog, turn. 38 sts.

Close spine

Row 65: Work the same as row 55. 21 sts.

Row 66: Sl, *k1, p1* 3 times, k1, p3, *k1, p1* 3 times, k1, p2tog, turn. 20 sts.

Switch to US 3 (3.25mm) circular needles. Join to work in the round, being careful not to twist. Place a marker at the beginning of the round.

Round 67: Sl, *p1, k1* 4 times, yo, k1, yo, *k1, p1* 4 times, k 2 tog, pick up 13 sts, cast on 7, pick up 13 sts. 54 sts.

Round 68: *K1, p1* 4 times, k2, yo, k1, yo, k2, *p1, k1* 20 times, p1. 56 sts.

Round 69: *K1, p1* 4 times, k3, yo, k1, yo, k3, *p1, k1* 20 times, p1. 58 sts.

Round 70: *K1, p1* 4 times, k4, yo, k1, yo, k4, *p1, k1* 20 times, p1. 60 sts.

Round 71: *K1, p1* 4 times, k5, yo, k1, yo, k5, *p1, k1* 20 times, p1. 62 sts.

Round 72: *K1, p1* 4 times, k6, yo, k1, yo, k6, *p1, k1* 20 times, p1. 64 sts.

Round 73: *K1, p1* 4 times, k7, yo, k1, yo, k7, *p1, k1* 20 times, p1. 66 sts.

Round 74: *K1, p1* 4 times, k8, yo, k1, yo, k8, *p1, k1* 20 times, p1. 68 sts.

Close spine

Round 75: *K1, p1* 4 times, k1, sl next 8 sts, fold right hand and left hand needles parallel to each other with wrong sides facing and points facing to the right (right needle is at the back), slip next st onto a crochet hook; it will be the 18th st in row. Insert crochet hook into 17th st (from the right needle) and pull this through the loop on hook. Rep. the same way from * to * as Close first spine (row 15), *k1, p1* 21 times. 52 sts.

Round 76: *K1, p1* 4 times, k3, *p1, k1* 20 times, p1. 52 sts.

Round 77: *K1, p1* 4 times, k1, yo, k1, yo, *k1, p1* 21 times. 54 sts.

Round 78: K2, yo, k2, yo, k6, yo, k1, yo, k6, yo, k2, yo, k11, yo, k2, yo, k11, yo, k2, yo, k9. 64 sts.

Round 79: K3, yo, k2, yo, k8, yo, k1, yo, k8, yo, k2, yo, k13, yo, k2, yo, k13, yo, k2, yo, k10. 74 sts.

Round 80: K4, yo, k2, yo, k10, yo, k1, yo, k10, yo, k2, yo, k15, yo, k2, yo, k15, yo, k2, yo, k11. 84 sts.

Round 81: K5, yo, k2, yo, k12, yo, k1, yo, k12, yo, k2, yo, k17, yo, k2, yo, k17, yo, k2, yo, k12. 94 sts.

Round 82: K6, yo, k2, yo, k14, yo, k1, yo, k14, yo, k2, yo, k19, yo, k2, yo, k19, yo, k2, yo, k13. 104 sts.

Round 83: K7, yo, k2, yo, k16, yo, k1, yo, k16, yo, k2, yo, k21, yo, k2, yo, k21, yo, k2, yo, k14. 114 sts.

Round 84: *K1, p1* 10 times, k8, yo, k1, yo, k8, *p1, k1* 38 times, p1. 116 sts.

Close spine

Round 85: *K1, p1* 10 times, k1, sl next 8 sts, fold right hand and left hand needles parallel to each other with wrong sides facing and points facing to the right (right needle is at the back), slip next st onto a crochet hook; it will be the 30th st in row.

Insert crochet hook into 29th st (from the right needle) and pull this through the loop on hook. Rep. the same way from * to * as Close first spine (row 15), *k1, p1* 39 times. 100 sts.

Rounds 86–89: K1, p1 rib.

Bind off. Weave in ends.

SIZE 12–24 MONTHS

Using a pair of US 3 (3.25mm) needles, cast on 61 sts.

Rows 1–6: K1, p1 rib.

Row 7: K30, yo, k1, yo, k30. 63 sts.

Row 8: P31, yo, p1, yo, p31. 65 sts.

Row 9: K32, yo, k1, yo, k32. 67 sts.

The dinky dragon hat encloses the head and neck but allows complete freedom of movement.

Row 10: P33, yo, p1, yo, p33. 69 sts.
Row 11: K34, yo, k1, yo, k34. 71 sts.
Row 12: P35, yo, p1, yo, p35. 73 sts.
Row 13: K36, yo, k1, yo, k36. 75 sts.
Row 14: P37, yo, p1, yo, p37. 77 sts.

Close spine (see page 139 for diagrams)
Row 15: K30, sl next 8 sts, fold right hand and left hand needles parallel to each other with wrong sides facing and points facing to the right (right needle is at the back), slip next st onto a crochet hook; it will be the 39th st in row. Insert crochet hook into 38th st (from the right needle) and pull this through the loop on hook. Continue in this way:
**pull next st from the left needle through st on hook,
pull next st from right needle through st on hook. **
Rep. from ** to ** until the last slipped st on the right needle has been pulled through the next st on the left needle, pull next st from the left needle through st on hook, slip this st back onto the left needle, unfold needles and hold normally, k31. 61 sts.
Row 16: Purl.
Rows 17-26: Rep. rows 7-16. 61 sts.
Rows 27-30: Rep. rows 7-10. 69 sts.
Row 31: K19, k2tog, k13, yo, k1, yo, k13, k2tog, turn. 69 sts.
Row 32: Sl, p14, yo, p1, yo, p14, p2tog, turn. 70 sts.
Row 33: Sl, k15, yo, k1, yo, k15, k2tog, turn. 71 sts.
Row 34: Sl, p16, yo, p1, yo, p16, p2tog, turn. 72 sts.

Close spine
Row 35: Sl, k9, sl next 8 sts, fold right hand and left hand needles parallel to each other with wrong sides facing and points facing to the right (right needle is at the back), slip next st onto a crochet hook; it will be the 19th st in row.
Insert crochet hook into 18th st (from the right needle) and pull this through the loop on hook. Rep. the same way from * to * as Close first spine (row 15), k10, k2tog, turn. 55 sts.
Row 36: Sl, p19, p2tog, turn. 54 sts.
Row 37: Sl, k9, yo, k1, yo, k9, k2tog, turn. 55 sts.
Row 38: Sl, p10, yo, p1, yo, p10, p2tog, turn. 56 sts.
Row 39: Sl, k11, yo, k1, yo, k11, k2tog, turn. 57 sts.
Row 40: Sl, p12, yo, p1, yo, p12, p2tog, turn. 58 sts.
Row 41: Sl, k13, yo, k1, yo, k13, k2tog, turn. 59 sts.
Rows 42-51: Rep. rows 32-41. 49 sts.
Rows 52-56: Rep. rows 32-36. 34 sts.
Row 57: Sl, *p1, k1* 4 times, p1, yo, k1, yo, p1, *k1, p1* 4 times, k2tog, turn. 35 sts.
Row 58: Sl, *k1, p1* 5 times, yo, p1, yo, *p1, k1* 5 times, p2tog, turn. 36 sts.
Row 59: Sl, *p1, k1* 4 times, p1, k2tog, yo, k1, yo, k2, p1, *k1, p1* 4 times, k2tog, turn. 37 sts.
Row 60: Sl, *k1, p1* 4 times, k1, p3, yo, p1, yo, p3, k1, *p1, k1* 4 times, p2tog, turn. 38 sts.
Row 61: Sl, *p1, k1* 4 times, p1, k4, yo, k1, yo, k4,
p1, *k1, p1* 4 times, k2tog, turn. 39 sts.
Row 62: Sl, *k1, p1* 4 times, k1, p5, yo, p1, yo, p5, k1, *p1, k1* 4 times, p2tog, turn. 40 sts.
Row 63: Sl, *p1, k1* 4 times, p1, k6, yo, k1, yo, k6, p1, *k1, p1* 4 times, k2tog, turn. 41 sts.
Row 64: Sl, *k1, p1* 4 times, k1, p7, yo, p1, yo, p7, k1, *p1, k1* 4 times, p2tog, turn. 42 sts.

Close spine
Row 65: Sl, *p1, k1* 4 times, p1, sl next 8 sts, fold right hand and left hand needles parallel to each other with wrong sides facing and points facing to the right (right needle is at the back), slip next st onto a crochet hook; it will be the 19th st in row.
Insert crochet hook into 18th st (from the right needle) and pull this through the loop on hook. Rep. the same way from * to * as Close first spine (row 15), *k1, p1* 5 times, k2tog, turn. 25 sts.
Row 66: Sl, *k1, p1* 9 times, k1, p2tog, turn. 24 sts.
Rows 67 and 68: Rep. rows 57 and 58. 26 sts.
Switch to US 3 (3.25mm) circular needles. Join to work in the round, being careful not to twist. Place a marker at the beginning of the round.
Round 69: Sl, *p1, k1* 4 times, p1, k2, yo, k1, yo, k2, p1, *k1, p1* 4 times, k2tog, pick up 12 sts, cast on 7 sts, pick up 12 sts. 58 sts.
Round 70: *K1, p1* 5 times, k3, yo, k1, yo, k3, *p1, k1* 20 times, p1. 60 sts.
Round 71: *K1, p1* 5 times, k4, yo, k1, yo, k4, *p1, k1* 20 times, p1. 62 sts.
Round 72: *K1, p1* 5 times, k5, yo, k1, yo, k5, *p1, k1* 20 times, p1. 64 sts.
Round 73: *K1, p1* 5 times, k6, yo, k1, yo, k6, *p1, k1* 20 times, p1. 66 sts.
Round 74: *K1, p1* 5 times, k7, yo, k1, yo, k7, *p1, k1* 20 times, p1. 68 sts.

Close spine
Round 75: *K1, p1* 5 times, sl next 8 sts, fold right hand and left hand needles parallel to each other with wrong sides facing and points facing to the right (right needle is at the back), slip next st onto a crochet hook; it will be the 19th st in row.
Insert crochet hook into 18th st (from the right needle) and pull this through the loop on hook. Rep. the same way from * to * as Close first spine (row 15), *k1, p1* 21 times. 52 sts.
Round 76: K1, p1 rib.
Round 77: *K1, p1* 5 times, yo, k1, yo, *p1, k1* 20 times, p1. 54 sts.
Round 78: *K1, p1* 5 times, k1, yo, k1, yo, k1, *p1, k1* 20 times, p1. 56 sts.
Round 79: *K1, p1* 5 times, k2, yo, k1, yo, k2, *p1, k1* 20 times, p1. 58 sts.
Rounds 80 and 81: Rep. rows 70 and 71. 62 sts.
Round 82: K3, yo, k2, yo, k10, yo, k1, yo, k10, yo, k2, yo, k11, yo, k2, yo, k11, yo, k2, yo, k8. 72 sts.
Round 83: K4, yo, k2, yo, k12, yo, k1, yo, k12, yo, k2, yo, k13, yo, k2, yo, k13, yo, k2, yo, k9. 82 sts.

Regular stockinette-stitch pattern of the main part of the hat.

Round 84: K5, yo, k2, yo, k14, yo, k1, yo, k14, yo, k2, yo, k15, yo, k2, yo, k15, yo, k2, yo, k10. 92 sts.
Close spine
Round 85: K6, yo, k2, yo, k8, sl next 8 sts, fold right hand and left hand needles parallel to each other with wrong sides facing and points facing to the right (right needle is at the back), slip next st onto a crochet hook; it will be the 27th st in row.
Insert crochet hook into 26th st (from the right needle) and pull this through the loop on hook. Rep. the same way from * to * as Close first spine (row 15), k9, yo, k2, yo, k17, yo, k2, yo, k17, yo, k2, yo, k11. 84 sts.
Round 86: K7, yo, k2, yo, k19, yo, k2, yo, k19, yo, k2, yo, k19, yo, k2, yo, k12. 92 sts.
Round 87: K8, yo, k2, yo, k10, yo, k1, yo, k10, yo, k2, yo, k21, yo, k2, yo, k21, yo, k2, yo, k13. 102 sts.
Round 88: K9, yo, k2, yo, k12, yo, k1, yo, k12, yo, k2, yo, k23, yo, k2, yo, k23, yo, k2, yo, k14. 112 sts.
Round 89: K10, yo, k2, yo, k14, yo, k1, yo, k14, yo, k2, yo, k25, yo, k2, yo, k25, yo, k2, yo, k15. 122 sts.
Round 90: *K1, p1* 13 times, k3, yo, k1, yo, k3, p1,

k1, p1 to end of round. 124 sts.
Round 91: *K1, p1* 13 times, k4, yo, k1, yo, k4, p1, *k1, p1* to end of round. 126 sts.
Round 92: *K1, p1* 13 times, k5, yo, k1, yo, k5, p1, *k1, p1* to end of round. 128 sts.
Round 93: *K1, p1* 13 times, k6, yo, k1, yo, k6, p1, *k1, p1* to end of round. 130 sts.
Round 94: *K1, p1* 13 times, k7, yo, k1, yo, k7, p1, *k1, p1* to end of round. 132 sts.
Close spine
Round 95: *K1, p1* 13 times, sl next 8 sts, fold right hand and left hand needles parallel to each other with wrong sides facing and points facing to the right (right needle is at the back), slip next st onto a crochet hook; it will be the 35th st in row.
Insert crochet hook into 34th st (from the right needle) and pull this through the loop on hook. Rep. the same way from * to * as Close first spine (row 15), *k1, p1* to end of round. 116 sts.
Bind off. Weave in ends.

SIZE 2-3 YEARS

Using a pair of US 3 (3.25mm) needles, cast on 65 sts.
Rows 1-6: K1, p1 rib.
Row 7: K32, yo, k1, yo, k32. 67 sts.
Row 8: P33), yo, p1, yo, p33. 69 sts.
Row 9: K34, yo, k1, yo, k34. 71 sts.
Row 10: P35, yo, p1, yo, p35. 73 sts.
Row 11: K36, yo, k1, yo, k36. 75 sts.
Row 12: P37, yo, p1, yo, p37. 77 sts.
Row 13: K38, yo, k1, yo, k38. 79 sts.
Row 14: P39, yo, p1, yo, p39. 81 sts.
Row 15: K32, sl next 8 sts, fold right hand and left hand needles parallel to each other with wrong sides facing and points facing to the right (right needle is at the back), slip next st onto a crochet hook; it will be the 41st st in row.
Insert crochet hook into 40th st (from the right needle) and pull this through the loop on hook.
*Continue in this way:
**pull next st from the left needle through st on hook,
pull next st from right needle through st on hook. **
Rep. from ** to ** until the last slipped st on the right needle has been pulled through the next st on the left needle, pull next st from the left needle through st on hook, slip this st back onto the left needle, unfold needles and hold normally*, K33. 65 sts.
Row 16: Purl.
Rows 17-26: Rep. rows 7-16. 65 sts.
Rows 27-32: Rep. rows 7-12. 77 sts.
Row 33: K21, k2tog, k15, yo, k1, yo, k15, k2tog, turn. 77 sts.
Row 34: Sl, p16, yo, p1, yo, p16, p2tog, turn. 78 sts.
Close spine
Row 35: Sl, k9, sl next 8 sts, fold right hand and

Follow this photo for the positioning of the spines.

left-hand needles parallel to each other with wrong sides facing and points facing to the right (right needle is at the back), slip next st onto a crochet hook; it will be the 19th st in row.

Insert crochet hook into 18th st (from the right needle) and pull this through the loop on hook. Rep. the same way from * to * as Close first spine (row 15), k10, k2tog, turn. 61 sts.

Row 36: Sl, p19, p2tog, turn. 60 sts.

Row 37: Sl, k9, yo, k1, yo, k9, k2tog, turn. 61 sts.

Row 38: Sl, k10, yo, p1, yo, p10, p2tog, turn. 62 sts.

Row 39: Sl, k11, yo, k1, yo, k11, k2tog, turn. 63 sts.

Row 40: Sl, p12, yo, p1, yo, p12, p2tog, turn. 64 sts.

Row 41: Sl, k13, yo, k1, yo, k13, k2tog, turn. 65 sts.

Row 42: Sl, p14, yo, p1, yo, p14, p2tog, turn. 66 sts.

Row 43: Sl, k15, yo, k1, yo, k15, k2tog, turn. 67 sts.

Rows 44-53: Rep. rows 34-43. 57 sts.

Rows 54-62: Rep. rows 34-42. 46 sts.

Row 63: Sl, *p1, k1* 4 times, p1, k6, yo, k1, yo, k6, p1, *k1, p1* 4 times, k2tog, turn. 47 sts.

Row 64: Sl, *k1, p1* 4 times, k1, p7, yo, p1, yo, p7, k1, *p1, k1* 4 times, p2tog, turn. 48 sts.

Close spine

Row 65: Sl, *p1, k1* 4 times, p1, sl next 8 sts, fold right hand and left hand needles parallel to each other with wrong sides facing and points facing to the right (right needle is at the back), slip next st onto a crochet hook; it will be the 19th st in row. Insert crochet hook into 18th st (from the right needle) and pull this through the loop on hook. Rep. the same way from * to * as Close first spine (row 15), *k1, p1* 5 times, k2tog, turn. 31 sts.

Row 66: Sl, *k1, p1* 9 times, k1, p2tog, turn. 30 sts.

Round 67: Sl, *p1, k1* 4 times, p1, yo, k1, yo, p1, *k1, p1* 4 times, k2tog, turn. 31 sts.

Round 68: Sl, *k1, p1* 5 times, yo, p1, yo, *p1, k1* 5 times, p2tog, turn. 32 sts.

Round 69: Sl, *p1, k1* 4 times, p1, k2, yo, k1, yo, k2, p1, *k1, p1* 4 times, k2tog, turn. 33 sts.

Round 70: Sl, *k1, p1* 4 times, k1, p3, yo, p1, yo, p3, k1, *p1, k1* 4 times, p2tog, turn. 34 sts.

Round 71: Sl, *p1, k1* 4 times, p1, k4, yo, k1, yo, k4, p1, *k1, p1* 4 times, k2tog, turn. 35 sts.

Round 72: Sl, *k1, p1* 4 times, k1, p5, yo, p1, yo, p5, k1, *p1, k1* 4 times, p2tog, turn. 36 sts.

Round 73: Sl, *p1, k1* 4 times, p1, k6, yo, k1, yo, k6, p1, *k1, p1* 4 times, k2tog, turn. 37 sts.

Round 74: Sl, *k1, p1* 4 times, k1, p7, yo, p1, yo, p7, k1, *p1, k1* 4 times, p2tog, turn. 38 sts.

Switch to US 3 (3.25mm) circular needles. Join to work in the round, being careful not to twist. Place a marker at the beginning of the round.

Close spine

Round 75: Sl, *p1, k1* 4 times, p1, sl next 8 sts, fold right hand and left hand needles parallel to each other with wrong sides facing and points facing to the right (right needle is at the back), slip next st onto a crochet hook; it will be the 19th st in row.

Insert crochet hook into 18th st (from the right

needle) and pull this through the loop on hook. Rep. the same way from * to * as Close first spine (row 15), *k1, p1* 5 times, k2tog, pick up 12 sts, cast on 7 sts, pick up 12 sts. 52 sts.

Round 76: K1, p1 rib.

Round 77: *K1, p1* 5 times, yo, k1, yo, p1, *k1, p1* 20 times. 54 sts.

Round 78: *K1, p1* 5 times, k1, yo, k1, yo, *k1, p1* 21 times. 56 sts.

Round 79: *K1, p1* 5 times, k2, yo, k1, yo, k2, p1, *k1, p1* 20 times. 58 sts.

Round 80: *K1, p1* 5 times, k3, yo, k1, yo, k3, p1,*k1, p1* 20 times. 60 sts.

Round 81: *K1, p1* 5 times, k4, yo, k1, yo, k4, p1,*k1, p1* 20 times. 62 sts.

Round 82: *K1, p1* 5 times, k5, yo, k1, yo, k5, p1,*k1, p1* 20 times. 64 sts.

Round 83: *K1, p1* 5 times, k6, yo, k1, yo, k6, p1,*k1, p1* 20 times. 66 sts.

Round 84: *K1, p1* 5 times, k7, yo, k1, yo, k7, p1,*k1, p1* 20 times. 68 sts.

Close spine

Round 85: *K1, p1* 5 times, sl next 8 sts, fold right hand and left hand needles parallel to each other with wrong sides facing and points facing to the right (right needle is at the back), slip next st in row.

Insert crochet hook into 18th st (from the right needle) and pull this through the loop on hook. Rep. the same way from * to * as Close first spine (row 15), *k1, p1* 21 times. 52 sts.

Rounds 86-89: Rep. rounds 76-79. 58 sts.

Round 90: K3, yo, k2, yo, k8, yo, k1, yo, k8, yo, k2, yo, k11, yo, k2, yo, k11, yo, k2, yo, k8. 68 sts.

Round 91: K4, yo, k2, yo, k10, yo, k1, yo, k10, yo, k2, yo, k13, yo, k2, yo, k13, yo, k2, yo, k9. 78 sts.

Round 92: K5, yo, k2, yo, k12, yo, k1, yo, k12, yo, k2, yo, k15, yo, k2, yo, k15, yo, k2, yo, k10. 88 sts.

Round 93: K6, yo, k2, yo, k14, yo, k1, yo, k14, yo, k2, yo, k17, yo, k2, yo, k17, yo, k2, yo, k11. 98 sts.

Round 94: K7, yo, k2, yo, k16, yo, k1, yo, k16, yo, k2, yo, k19, yo, k2, yo, k19, yo, k2, yo, k12. 108 sts.

Close spine

Round 95: K8, yo, k2, yo, k10, sl next 8 sts, fold right hand and left hand needles parallel to each other with wrong sides facing and points facing to the right (right needle is at the back), slip next st onto a crochet hook; it will be the 31st st in row. Insert crochet hook into 30th st (from the right needle) and pull this through the loop on hook. Rep. the same way from * to * as Close first spine (row 15), k11, yo, k2, yo, k21, yo, k2, yo, k21, yo, k2, yo, k13. 100 sts.

Round 96: K9, yo, k2, yo, k23, yo, k2, yo, k23, yo, k2, yo, k23, yo, k2, yo, k14. 108 sts.

Round 97: K10, yo, k2, yo, k12, yo, k1, yo ,k12, yo, k2, yo, k25, yo, k2, yo, k25, yo, k2, yo, k15. 118 sts.

Round 98: K11, yo, k2, yo, k14, yo, k1, yo, k14, yo, k2, yo, k27, yo, k2, yo, k27, yo, k2, yo, k16. 128 sts.

Round 99: K12, yo, k2, yo, k16, yo, k1, yo, k16, yo, k2, yo, k29, yo, k2, yo, k29, yo, k2, yo, k17. 138 sts.
Round 100: *K1, p1* 15 times, k3, yo, k1, yo, k3, p1, *k1, p1* to end of round. 140 sts.
Round 101: *K1, p1* 15 times, k4, yo, k1, yo, k4, p1, *k1, p1* to end of round. 142 sts.
Round 102: *K1, p1* 15 times, k5, yo, k1, yo, k5, p1, *k1, p1* to end of round. 144 sts.
Round 103: *K1, p1* 15 times, k6, yo, k1, yo, k6, p1, *k1, p1* to end of round. 146 sts.
Round 104: *K1, p1* 15 times, k7, yo, k1, yo, k7, p1, *k1, p1* to end of round. 148 sts.
Close spine
Round 105: *K1, p1* 15 times, sl next 8 sts, fold right hand and left hand needles parallel to each other with wrong sides facing and points facing to the right (right needle is at the back), slip next st onto a crochet hook; it will be the 39th st in row.
Insert crochet hook into 38th st (from the right needle) and pull this through the loop on hook. Rep. the same way from * to * as Close first spine (row 15), *k1, p1* to end of round. 132 sts. Bind off. Weave in ends.

MITTENS

LEFT MITTEN

Cuff

Using US 0 (2mm) double-pointed needles, cast on 22 (24, 26) sts and divide evenly among 3 needles. Join to work in the round, being careful not to twist. Place a marker at the beginning of the round.
Rounds 1-10 (1-12, 1-14): Work in k1, p1 rib.

Thumb gusset

Switch to US 3 (3.25mm) double-pointed needles to work rest of mitten.
Round 1: M1R, k5 (5, 6), yo, k1, yo, k15 (17, 18). 25 (27, 29) sts.
Round 2: K8 (8, 9), yo, k1, yo, k16 (18, 19). 27 (29, 31) sts.
Round 3: M1R, k1, M1L, k6 (6, 7), yo, k1, yo, k17 (19, 20). 31 (33, 35) sts.
Round 4: K12 (12, 13), yo, k1, yo, k18 (20, 21). 33 (35, 37) sts.
Round 5: M1R, k3, M1L, k8 (8, 9), yo, k1, yo, k19 (21, 22). 37 (39, 41) sts.
Close first spine (see page 139 for diagrams)
Round 6: K11 (11, 12), sl next 5 (5, 5) sts, fold right hand and left hand needles parallel to each other with wrong sides facing and points facing to the right (right needle is at the back), slip next st onto a crochet hook; it will be the 17th (17th, 18th) st in row.
Insert crochet hook into 16th (16th, 17th) st (from the right needle) and pull this through the loop

on hook. *Continue in this way:
**pull next st from the left needle through st on hook,
pull next st from right needle through st on hook. **
Rep. from ** to ** until the last slipped st on the right needle has been pulled through the next st on the left needle, pull next st from the left needle through st on hook, slip this st back onto the left needle, unfold needles and hold normally*, k16 (18, 19). 27 (29, 31) sts.
Round 7: M1R, k5, M1L, k20 (22, 24). 29 (31, 33) sts.
Round 8: K13 (13, 14), yo, k1, yo, k15 (17, 18). 31 (33, 35) sts.
Round 9 (9, 9) (two larger sizes only): M1R, k7, M1L, k (5, 6), yo, k1, yo, k (18, 19). (37, 39) sts.
Round 9 (10, 10): K1, place7 (9, 9) thumb sts on waste yarn, rejoin to work hand sts in the round, k6 (7, 8), yo, k1, yo, k16 (19, 20). 26 (30, 32) sts.
Round 10 (11, 11): K8 (9, 10), yo, k1, yo, k17 (20, 21). 28 (32, 34) sts.
Round 11 (small size only): K9, yo, k1, yo, k18. 30 sts.
Round 12 (12, 12) (all sizes): K10 (10, 11), yo, k1, yo, k19 (21, 22). 32 (34, 36) sts.
Close spine
Round 13 (13, 13): K6 (6, 7), sl next 5 (5, 5) sts, fold right hand and left hand needles parallel to each other with wrong sides facing and points facing to the right (right needle is at the back), slip next st onto a crochet hook; it will be the 12th (12th, 13th) st in row.
Insert crochet hook into 11th (11th, 12th) st (from the right needle) and pull this through the loop on hook. Rep. the same way from * to * as Close first spine (round 6), k16 (18, 19). 22 (24, 26) sts.
Round 14 (14, 14): Knit.
Round 15 (15, 15): K6 (6, 7), yo, k1, yo, k15 (17, 18). 24 (26, 28) sts.
Round 16 (16, 16): K7 (7, 8), yo, k1, yo, k16 (18, 19). 26 (28, 30) sts.
Round 17 (17, 17): K8 (8, 9), yo, k1, yo, k17 (19, 20). 28 (30, 32) sts.
Round 18 (18, 18): K9 (9, 10), yo, k1, yo, k18 (20, 21). 30 (32, 34) sts.
Round 19 (19, 19): K10 (10, 11), yo, k1, yo, k19 (21, 22). 32 (34, 36) sts.
Round 20 (20, 20): Rep. round 13 (13, 13). 22 (24, 26) sts.
Rounds 21 (21, 21)-22 (26, 28): Knit.
Closing up the top
Round 23 (27, 29): K2tog to end of round. 11 (12, 13) sts.
Round 24 (28, 30): Knit.
Round 25 (29, 31): K2tog to end of round. (If you get to the end of the round with only one stitch left, knit it.) 6 (6, 7) sts.
Cut a tail long enough to weave in. Pull it through all the stitches; remove them from the needles. Pull the tail tightly and secure. Weave in ends.

Thumb

Place 7 (9, 9) stitches from waste yarn onto US 3 (3.25mm) double-pointed needles. Rejoin yarn and pick up one extra stitch in the corner where the mitten meets the gusset. 8 (10, 10) sts.
Rounds 1-6 (1-6, 1-8): Knit.
Round 7 (7, 9): K2tog to end of round. 4 (5, 5) sts.
Finish as for Closing up the top.

RIGHT MITTEN

Cuff

Using US 0 (2mm) double-pointed needles, cast on 22 (24, 26) sts and divide evenly among 3 needles. Join to work in the round, being careful not to twist. Place a marker at the beginning of the round.
Rounds 1-10 (1-12, 1-14): Work in k1, p1 rib.

Thumb gusset

Switch to US 3 (3.25mm) double-pointed needles to work rest of mitten.
Round 1: K15 (17, 18), yo, k1, yo, k5 (5, 6), M1R. 25 (27, 29) sts.
Round 2: K16 (18, 19), yo, k1, yo, k8 (8, 9). 27 (29, 31) sts.
Round 3: K17 (19, 20), yo, k1, yo, k6 (6, 7), M1L, k1, M1R. 31 (33, 35) sts.
Round 4: K18 (20, 21), yo, k1, yo, k12 (12, 13). 33 (35, 37) sts.
Round 5: K19 (21, 22), yo, k1, yo, k8 (8, 9), M1L, k3, M1R. 37 (39, 41) sts.
Close first spine
Round 6: K16 (18, 19), sl next 5 sts, fold right hand and left hand needles parallel to each other with wrong sides facing and points facing to the right (right needle is at the back), slip next st onto a crochet hook; it will be the 22nd (24th, 25th) st in row.
Insert crochet hook into 21st (23rd, 24th) st (from the right needle) and pull this through the loop on hook. *Continue in this way:
**pull next st from the left needle through st on hook,
pull next st from right needle through st on hook. **
Rep. from ** to ** until the last slipped st on the right needle has been pulled through the next st on the left needle, pull next st from the left needle through st on hook, slip this st back onto the left needle, unfold needles and hold normally*, k11 (11, 12). 27 (29, 31) sts.
Round 7: K20 (22, 24), M1L, k5, M1R. 29 (31, 33) sts.
Round 8: K15 (17, 18), yo, k1, yo, k13 (13, 14). 31 (33, 35) sts.
Round (9, 9) (two larger sizes only): K (18, 19), yo, k1, yo, k (5, 6), M1L, k7, M1R. (37, 39) sts.
Round 9 (10, 10): K16 (19, 20), yo, k1, yo, k6 (7, 8), place 7 (9, 9) thumb sts on waste yarn, rejoin to work hand sts in the round, k1. 26 (30, 32) sts.

Round 10 (11, 11): K17 (20, 21), yo, k1, yo, k8 (9, 10). 28 (32, 34) sts.
Round 11 (small size only): K18, yo, k1, yo, k9. 30 sts.
Round 12 (12, 12) (all sizes): K19 (21, 22), yo, k1, yo, k10 (10, 11). 32 (34, 36) sts.
Close spine
Round 13 (13, 13): K16 (18, 19), sl next 5 (5, 5) sts, fold right hand and left hand needles parallel to each other with wrong sides facing and points facing to the right (right needle is at the back), slip next st onto a crochet hook; it will be the 22nd (24th, 25th) st in row.
Insert crochet hook into 21st (23rd, 24th) st (from the right needle) and pull this through the loop on hook. Rep. the same way from * to * as Close first spine (round 6), k6 (6,7). 22 (24, 26) sts.
Round 14 (14, 14): Knit.
Round 15 (15, 15): K15 (17, 18), yo, k1, yo, k6 (6, 7). 24 (26, 28) sts.
Round 16 (16, 16): K16 (18, 19), yo, k1, yo, k7 (7, 8). 26 (28, 30) sts.
Round 17 (17, 17): K17 (19, 20), yo, k1, yo, k8 (8, 9). 28 (30, 32) sts.
Round 18 (18, 18): K18 (20, 21), yo, k1, yo, k9 (9, 10). 30 (32, 34) sts.
Round 19 (19, 19): K19 (21, 22), yo, k1, yo, k10 (10, 11). 32 (34, 36) sts.

Round 20 (20, 20): Rep. round 13 (13, 13). 22 (24, 26) sts.
Rounds 21 (21, 21)-22 (26, 28): Knit.
Closing up the top
Round 23 (27, 29): K2tog to end of round. 11 (12, 13) sts.
Round 24 (28, 30): Knit.
Round 25 (29, 31): K2tog to end of round. (If you get to the end of the round with only one stitch left, knit it.) 6 (6, 7) sts.
Finish as for left mitten Closing up the top.

Thumb

Place 7 (9, 9) stitches from waste yarn onto US 3 (3.25mm) double-pointed needles. Rejoin yarn and pick up one extra stitch in the corner where the mitten meets the gusset. 8 (10, 10) sts.
Rounds 1-6 (1-6, 1-8): Knit.
Round 7 (7 9): K2tog to end of round. 4 (5, 5) sts.
Finish as for left mitten Closing up the top.

Dinky dragon mittens with their little spines.

adorable animals

darling panda

The panda hat, mittens, and booties are straightforward to knit and look incredibly cute. You'll knit the eyes and ears and use embroidery for the nose and pupils.

COVERALL HAT,
MITTENS, AND BOOTIES
LEVEL: intermediate
SIZES
6-12 months (12-24 months, 2-3 years)
Finished measurements
From "cheek to cheek" around the hat:
14 (14.5, 15)in. (36 [37, 38]cm)
Mitten circumference: 5½ (6, 6½)in.
(13.75 [15, 16.25]cm)
Mitten length: 5½ (6½, 7)in.
(14 [16.5, 18]cm)
Booties heel to toe:
3 (3 ³/₅, 4)in. (7.5 [9, 11]cm)
MATERIALS
HAT
Yarn:
Color A: 1 x 3oz (85g) ball (135yd/123m)
Lion Brand Jiffy Yarn, 100% acrylic,
White
Color B: 1 x 3oz (85g) ball (135yd/123m) Lion
Brand Jiffy Yarn, 100% acrylic,
Black
Needles:
• 1 pair of US 3 (3.25mm) needles
• US 3 (3.25mm) circular needles
• Stitch marker
• US C-2 (2.75mm) crochet hook
• Yarn needle

MITTENS
Main yarn:
Color A: 1 x 3oz (85g) ball (135yd/123m) Lion
Brand Jiffy Yarn, 100% acrylic, Black
Small amount:
Color B: Lion Brand Jiffy Yarn, 100% acrylic,
White
Needles:
• 4 x US 0 (2mm) double-pointed needles
• 4 x US 3 (3.25mm) double-pointed needles
• US C-2 (2.75mm) crochet hook
• Yarn needle
BOOTIES
Main yarn:
Color A: 1 x 3oz (85g) ball (135yd/123m) Lion
Brand Jiffy Yarn, 100% acrylic, Black
Small amount:
Color B: Lion Brand Jiffy Yarn, 100% acrylic,
White
Needles:
• 4 x US 3 (3.25mm) double-pointed needles
• US C-2 (2.75mm) crochet hook
• Yarn needle
GAUGE
16 sts and 25 rows. 4in./10cm square in
stockinette stitch worked with US 3 (3.25mm)
needles.
19 sts and 28 rows. 4in./10cm square in k1, p1
rib worked with US 3 (3.25mm) needles.

HAT

Using a pair of US 3 (3.25mm) needles and A,
cast on 57 (61, 65) sts.
Rows 1-6 (6, 6): K1, p1 rib.
Rows 7- 30 (30, 32): Work in stockinette stitch,
starting with a k row.
Row 31 (31, 33): K18 (19, 21), k2tog, k17 (19, 19),
k2tog, turn. 55 (59, 63) sts.
Row 32 (32, 34): Sl, p17 (19, 19), p2tog, turn. 54
(58, 62) sts.
Row 33 (33, 35): Sl, k17 (19, 19), k2tog, turn. 53
(57, 61) sts.
Rep. rows 32 (32, 34) and 33 (33, 35) to row 54
(56, 62). 32 (34, 34) sts.
Row 55 (57, 63): Sl, *p1, k1* rep. from * to * 8 (9,
9) times, p1, k2tog, turn. 31 (33, 33) sts.
Row 56 (58, 64): Sl, *k1, p1* rep. from * to * 8
(9, 9) times, k1, p2tog, turn. 30 (32, 32) sts.
Rep. rows 55 (57, 63) and 56 (58, 64) to row 66
(68, 74). 20 (22, 22) sts.

Neck ruff

Switch to US 3 (3.25mm) circular needles and B.
Place a marker at the beginning of the round.
Round 67 (69, 75): Sl, *p1, k1* rep. from * to * 8
(9, 9) times, p1, k2tog, pick up 13 (12, 12) sts on
one side of the hat, cast on 7 (7, 7) sts, join to
work in the round, being careful not to twist,
pick up 13 (12, 12) sts on the other side of the hat.
52 (52, 52) sts.
Rounds 68-77 (70-81, 76-89): K1, p1 rib.
Round 78 (82, 90): K2 (3, 3), yo, k2, yo, k11 (11, 11),
yo, k2, yo, k11 (11, 11), yo, k2, yo, k11 (11, 11), yo, k2, yo,
k9 (8, 8). 60 (60, 60) sts.
Round 79 (83, 91): K3 (4, 4), yo, k2, yo, k13 (13,
13), yo, k2, yo, k13 (13, 13), yo, k2, yo, k13 (13, 13),
yo, k2, yo, k10 (9, 9). 68 (68, 68) sts.
Round 80 (84, 92): K4 (5, 5), yo, k2, yo, k15 (15,
15), yo, k2, yo, k15 (15, 15), yo, k2, yo, k15 (15, 15),
yo, k2, yo, k11 (10, 10). 76 (76, 76) sts.
Round 81 (85, 93): K5 (6, 6), yo, k2, yo, k17 (17,
17), yo, k2, yo, k17 (17, 17), yo, k2, yo, k17 (17, 17), yo,
k2, yo, k12 (11, 11). 84 (84, 84) sts.
Round 82 (86, 94): K6 (7, 7), yo, k2, yo, k19 (19,
19), yo, k2, yo, k19 (19, 19), yo, k2, yo, k19 (19, 19),
yo, k2, yo, k13 (12, 12). 92 (92, 92) sts.
Round 83 (87, 95): K7 (8, 8), yo, k2, yo, k21 (21,
21), yo, k2, yo, k21 (21, 21), yo, k2, yo, k21 (21, 21),
yo, k2, yo, k14 (13, 13). 100 (100, 100) sts.
Round (88, 96) (two larger sizes only): K (9, 9),
yo, k2, yo, k (23, 23), yo, k2, yo, k (23, 23), yo, k2,
yo, k (23, 23), yo, k2, yo, k (14, 14). (108, 108) sts.

The long cuffs on the mittens keep
hands and wrists warm.

The two-tone mittens complement the hat beautifully.

Round (89, 97) (two larger sizes only): K (10, 10), yo, k2, yo, k (25, 25), yo, k2, yo, k (25, 25), yo, k2, yo, k (25, 25), yo, k2, yo, k (15, 15). (116, 116) sts.
Round (98) (largest size only): K (11), yo, k2, yo, k (27), yo, k2, yo, k (27), yo, k2, yo, k (27), yo, k2, yo, k (16). (124) sts.
Round (99) (largest size only): K (12), yo, k2, yo, k (29), yo, k2, yo, k (29), yo, k2, yo, k (29), yo, k2, yo, k (17). (132) sts.
Rounds 84-89 (90-95, 100-105) (all sizes): K1, p1 rib.
Bind off. Weave in ends.

Ears (make 2)

Using a pair of US 3 (3.25mm) needles and B, cast on 23 sts, leaving an 8in./20cm tail for sewing the ears in place.
Rows 1-5: K1, p1 rib.
Cut tail long enough to weave in. Pull through all 23 stitches and remove them from needle. Pull the tail tightly and secure. Make a strong knot.

Eyes (make 2)

With a US C-2 (2.75mm) crochet hook and B, ch4. Join with sl st to form ring.
Row 1: Ch3, 13dc in ring, join with sl st on top of the first 3ch stitches. 14dc.
Finish off, leaving a long tail for sewing.

FINISHING

1 Using B, embroider the nose in the middle of the hat's rib, at approximately the third and fourth rows. The nose is made of three straight lines: long, medium, and short.
2 Sew the ears to the hat in the position shown.
3 Sew the eyes to the hat as shown and embroider two small pupils in satin stitch, one for each eye, using A.
4 Weave in ends.

MITTENS

(MAKE 2)

Cuff

Using US 0 (2mm) double-pointed needles and B, cast on 22 (24, 26) sts and divide evenly among 3 needles. Join to work in the round, being careful not to twist. Place a marker at the beginning of the round.
Rounds 1-10 (1-12, 1-14): Work in k1, p1 rib.

Thumb gusset

Switch to US 3 (3.25mm) double-pointed needles to work rest of mitten.
Round 1: M1R, knit to end of round. 23 (25, 27) sts.
Round 2: Knit.
Round 3: M1R, k1, M1L, knit to end of round. 25 (27, 29) sts.
Round 4: Knit.
Round 5: M1R, k3, M1L, knit to end of round. 27 (29, 31) sts.
Round 6: Knit.
Round 7: M1R, k5, M1L, knit to end of round. 29 (31, 33) sts.
Round 8: Knit.
Round 9 (two larger sizes only): M1R, k7, M1L, knit to end of round. (33, 35) sts.
Round 9 (9, 9) (10, 10): K1, place 7 (9, 9) thumb stitches on waste yarn. Rejoin to work hand stitches in the round, k21 (23, 25). 22 (24, 26) sts. Switch to A.
Rounds 10-22 (11-26, 11-28): Knit.
Closing up the top
Round 23 (27, 29): K2tog to end of round. 11 (12, 13) sts.
Round 24 (28, 30): Knit.
Round 25 (29, 31): K2tog to end of round. (If you

get to the end of the round with only one stitch left, knit it.) 6 (6, 7) sts.

Cut a tail long enough to weave in. Pull it through all the stitches and remove them from the needles. Pull the tail tightly and secure. Weave in ends.

Thumb

Switch to B.

Place 7 (9, 9) stitches from waste yarn onto US 3 (3.25mm) double-pointed needles. Rejoin yarn and pick up one extra stitch in the corner where the mitten meets the gusset. Place a marker at the beginning of the round. 8 (10, 10) sts.

Rounds 1-6 (1-6, 1-8): Knit.

Round 7 (7, 9): K2tog to end of round. 4 (5, 5) sts.
Finish as for mitten Closing up the top.

Eyes and ears (make 8)

With a US C-2 (2.75mm) crochet hook and B: ch4.
Join with sl st to form ring.

Round 1: 7sc into ring.
End with sl st in next st to join.
Fasten off, leaving a tail long enough for sewing.

FINISHING

1 Sew the eyes onto the mittens.
2 With A embroider two small pupils (highlights) in satin stitch.
3 Sew the ears onto the mittens.
4 With B embroider the nose in satin stitch.
5 Weave in ends.

BOOTIES

(MAKE 2)

Using US 3 (3.25mm) double-pointed needles and B, cast on 24 (26, 28) sts and divide evenly among 3 double-pointed needles. Join to work in the round, being careful not to twist. Place a marker at the beginning of the round.

Rounds 1-10 (1-12, 1-14): Work in k1, p1 rib.
Rounds 11-13 (13-15, 15-17): Knit.

Heel

Row 14 (16, 18): K12 (13, 14), turn.
Row 15 (17, 19): P12 (13, 14), turn.
Rep. rows 14 (16, 18) and 15 (17, 19) to row 19 (21, 23).
Row 20 (22, 24): K2, k2tog, k4 (5, 6), k2tog, turn. 22 (24, 26) sts.
Row 21 (23, 25): Sl, p4 (5, 6), p2tog, turn. 21 (23, 25) sts.
Row 22 (24, 26): Sl, k4 (5, 6), k2tog, turn. 20 (22, 24) sts.
Row 23 (25, 27): Sl, p4 (5, 6), p2tog, turn. 19 (21, 23) sts.
Work in rounds from now on.
Row 24 (26, 28): Sl, k4 (5, 6), k2tog, pick up 3 sts down side of heel, k12 (13, 14). 21 (23, 25) sts.
Row 25 (27, 29): Pick up 3 sts up side of heel, k21 (23, 25). 24 (26, 28) sts.
Rounds 26-28 (28-34, 30-40): Knit.
Switch to A.
Rounds 29-40 (35-46, 41- 52): Knit.

Closing up the toe

Round 41 (47, 53): K2tog to end of round. 12 (13, 14) sts.
Round 42 (48, 54): Knit.
Round 43 (49, 55): K2tog to end of round. (If you get to the end of the round with only one stitch left, knit it.) 6 (7, 7) sts.
Cut a tail long enough to weave in. Pull through all stitches and remove them from the needles. Pull the tail tightly and secure.

Eyes and ears (make 8)

Make the same as for the Mittens.

FINISHING

1 Sew the eyes onto the booties.
2 With A embroider two small pupils (highlights) in satin stitch.
3 Sew the ears onto the booties.
4 With B embroider the nose in satin stitch.
5 Weave in ends.

Perfect for winter evenings at home, the little booties complete the outfit.

cute shark

This adorable hat with matching mittens has dramatic shark features that are sure to appeal to your child. There are crochet details on both garments.

COVERALL HAT AND MITTENS
LEVEL: advanced
SIZES
6-12 months (12-24 months, 2-3 years)
Finished measurements
HAT
From "cheek to cheek" around the hat:
14 (14½, 15)in. (36 [37, 38]cm)
Mitten circumference: 5½ (6, 6½)in.
(13.75 [15, 16.25]cm)
Mitten length: 5½ (6½, 7)in. (14 [16.5, 18cm)
MATERIALS
HAT
Main yarn:
Color A: 1 x 3oz (85g) ball (135yd/123m) Lion Brand Jiffy Yarn, 100% acrylic, Heather Blue, 5 Bulky
Small amounts:
Color B: Lion Brand Pound of Love Baby Yarn, 100% acrylic, White, 4 Medium
Color C: Lion Brand Jiffy Yarn, 100% acrylic, White, 5 Bulky
Color D: Lion Brand Jiffy Yarn, 100% acrylic, Black
Needles:
• 1 pair of US 3 (3.25mm) needles
• US 3 (3.25mm) circular needle
• Yarn needle to weave in ends

• 3mm crochet hook
• 1 pair of US 0 (2mm) double-pointed needles
• 1 pair of US 3 (3.25mm) double-pointed needles
• Small amount of toy stuffing
MITTENS
Main yarn:
Color A: 1 x 3oz (85g) ball (135yd/123m) Lion Brand Jiffy Yarn, 100% acrylic, Heather Blue, 5 Bulky
Small amounts:
Color B: Lion Brand Pound of Love Baby Yarn, 100% acrylic, White, 4 Medium
Color C: Lion Brand Jiffy Yarn, 100% acrylic, White, 5 Bulky
Color D: Lion Brand Jiffy Yarn, 100% acrylic, Black, 5 Bulky
Needles:
• 1 pair of US 0 (2mm) double-pointed needles
• 1 pair of US 3 (3.25mm) needles
• 3mm crochet hook
• Yarn needle to weave in ends
GAUGE
16 sts and 25 rows = 4in./10cm square in stockinette stitch, worked with US 3 (3.25mm) needles.
19 sts and 28 rows = 4in./10cm square in k1, p1 rib, worked with US 3 (3.25mm) needles.

HAT

Using a pair of US 3 (3.25mm) needles and A, cast on 57 (61, 65) sts.
Rows 1-6: K1, p1 rib.
Rows 7-10: Work in stockinette st.
Shape large middle fin
Row 11: K28 (30, 32), yo, k1, yo, k28 (30, 32. (59 (63, 67) sts.
Row 12: P29 (31, 33), yo, p1, yo, p29 (31, 33). 61 (65, 69) sts.
Row 13: K30 (32, 34), yo, k1, yo, k30 (32, 34). 63 (67, 71) sts.
Row 14: P31 (33, 35), yo, p1 (1, 1), yo, p31 (33, 35). 65 (69, 73) sts.
Row 15: K32 (34, 36), yo, k1, yo, k32 (34, 36). 67 (71, 75) sts.
Row 16: P33 (35, 37), yo, p1, yo, p33 (35, 37). 69 (73, 77) sts.
Row 17: K34 (36, 38), yo, k1, yo, k34 (36, 38). 71 (75, 79) sts.
Row 18: P35 (37, 39), yo, p1, yo, p35 (37, 39). 73 (77, 81) sts.
Shape two small side fins
Row 19: K15 (15, 15), yo, k1, yo, k20 (22, 24), yo, k1, yo, k20 (22, 24), yo, k1, yo, k15 (15, 15). 79 (83, 87) sts.
Row 20: P16 (16, 16), yo, p1, yo, p22 (24, 26), yo, p1, yo, p22 (24, 26), yo, p1, yo, p16 (16, 16). 85 (89, 93) sts.
Row 21: K17 (17, 17), yo, k1, yo, k24 (26, 28), yo, k1, yo, k24 (26, 28), yo, k1, yo, k17 (17, 17). 91 (95, 99) sts.
Row 22: P18 (18, 18), yo, p1, yo, p26 (28, 30), yo, p1, yo, p26 (28, 30), yo, p1, yo, p18 (18, 18). 97 (101, 105) sts.
Row 23: K19 (19, 19), yo, k1, yo, k28 (30, 32), yo, k1, yo, k28 (30, 32), yo, k1, yo, k19 (19, 19). 103 (107, 111) sts.
Row 24: P20 (20, 20), yo, p1, yo, p30 (32, 34), yo, p1, yo, p30 (32, 34), yo, p1, yo, p20 (20, 20). 109 (113, 117) sts.
Row 25: K21 (21, 21), yo, k1, yo, k32 (34, 36), yo, k1, yo, k32 (34, 36), yo, k1, yo, k21 (21, 21). 115 (119, 123) sts.
Row 26: P22 (22, 22), yo, p1, yo, p34 (36, 38), yo, p1, yo, p34 (36, 38), yo, p1, yo, p22 (22, 22). 121 (125, 129) sts.
Close small fins (see page 139 for diagrams)
Row 27: K15 (15, 15), sl next 8 sts, fold right-hand and left-hand needles parallel to each other with wrong sides facing and points facing to the right (right needle is at the back), slip next st onto a crochet hook; it will be 24th st in row.

Cute shark looks delightful from both the back and the front! Refer to the picture on the right to sew on the eyes.

Insert crochet hook into 23rd st (from the right needle) and pull this through the loop on the hook. Continue in this way:

**pull next st from the left needle through st on hook,

pull next st from right needle through st on hook, **

rep. from ** to ** until the last slipped st on the right needle has been pulled through the next st on the left needle, pull next st from the left needle through st on hook, slip this st back onto the left needle, unfold needles and hold normally, k29 (31, 33), yo, k1, yo, k28 (30, 32), sl next 8 sts, fold right hand and left hand needles parallel to each other with wrong sides facing and points facing to the right (right needle is at the back), slip next st onto a crochet hook. Repeat the same way as the first small fin until the last slipped st on the right needle has been pulled through the next st on the left needle, pull next st from the left needle through st on

hook, slip this st back onto the left needle, unfold needles and hold normally, k16 (16, 16). 91 (95, 99) sts.

Row 28: P45 (47, 49), yo, p1, yo, p45 (47, 49). 93 (97, 105) sts.

Close large fin

Row 29: K28 (30, 32), sl next 18 (18, 18) sts, fold right-hand and left-hand needles parallel to each other with wrong sides facing and points facing to the right (right needle is at the back), slip next st onto a crochet hook; it will be the 47th (49th, 51st) st in row.

Insert crochet hook into 46th (48th, 50th) st (from the right needle) and pull this through the loop on hook. Continue in this way:

**pull next st from the left needle through st on hook,

pull next st from right needle through st on hook, **

rep. from ** to ** until the last slipped st on the right needle has been pulled through the next st on the left needle, pull next st from the left needle through st on hook, slip this st back onto the left needle, unfold needles and hold normally, K29 (31, 33). 57 (61, 65) sts.

Row 30: P57 (61, 65). 57 (61, 65) sts.

Largest size only:

Row 31: K65.

Row 32: P65.

All sizes:

Row 31 (31, 33): K18 (19, 21), k2tog, k17 (19, 19), k2tog, sl, turn. 55 (59, 63) sts.

Row 32 (32, 34): P17 (19, 19), p2tog, sl, turn. 54 (58, 62) sts.

Row 33 (33, 35): K17 (19, 19), k2tog, sl, turn. 53 (57, 61) sts.

Rep. rows 32 (32, 34) and 33 (33, 35) to row 54 (56, 62). 32 (34, 34) sts.

Row 55 (57, 63): *P1, k1* rep. from * to * 8 (9, 9) times, p1, k2tog, sl, turn. 31 (33, 33) sts.

Row 56 (58, 64): * K1, p1 * rep. from * to * 8 (9, 9) times, k1, p2tog, sl, turn. 30 (32, 32) sts.

Rep. to row 66 (68, 74). 20 (22, 22) sts.

Neck ruff

Switch to a circular needle and place marker to mark the beginning of the row.

Round 67 (69, 75): sl, *P1, k1* rep. from * to * 8 (9, 9) times, p1, k2tog, pick up 13 (12, 12) sts on one side of the hat, cast on 7 (7, 7) sts, join to work in the round, being careful not to twist, pick up 13 (12, 12) sts on the other side of the hat. 52 (52, 52) sts.

Round 78 (82, 90): K2 (3, 3), yo, k2, yo, k11 (11, 11), yo, k2, yo, k11 (11, 11), yo, k2, yo, k11 (11, 11), yo, k2, yo, k9 (8, 8). 60 (60, 60) sts.

Round 79 (83, 91): K3 (4, 4), yo, k2, yo, k13 (13, 13), yo, k2, yo, k13 (13, 13), yo, k2, yo, k13 (13, 13), yo, k2, yo, k10 (9, 9). 68 (68, 68) sts.

Round 80 (84, 92): K4 (5, 5), yo, k2, yo, k15 (15,

Children will love the mini-fins on the mittens.

The neck ruff fits snugly around the child's head but feels soft against the skin.

15), yo, k2, yo, k15 (15, 15), yo, k2, yo, k15 (15, 15), yo, k2, yo, k11 (10, 10). 76 (76, 76) sts.

Round 81 (85, 93): K5 (6, 6), yo, k2, yo, k17 (17, 17), yo, k2, yo, k17 (17, 17), yo, k2, yo, k17 (17, 17), yo, k2, yo, k12 (11, 11). 84 (84, 84) sts.

Round 82 (86, 94): K6 (7, 7), yo, k2, yo, k19 (19, 19), yo, k2, yo, k19 (19, 19), yo, k2, yo, k19 (19, 19), yo, k2, yo, k13 (12, 12). 92 (92, 92) sts.

Round 83 (87, 95): K7 (8, 8), yo, k2, yo, k21 (21, 21), yo, k2, yo, k21 (21, 21), yo, k2, yo, k21 (21, 21), yo, k2, yo, k14 (13, 13). 100 (100, 100) sts.

Round (88, 96) (two larger sizes only): K (9, 9), yo, k2, yo, k (23, 23), yo, k2, yo, k (23, 23), yo, k2, yo, k (23, 23), yo, k2, yo, k (14, 14). (108, 108) sts.

Round (89, 97) (two larger sizes only): K (10, 10), yo, k2, yo, k (25, 25), yo, k2, yo, k (25, 25), yo, k2, yo, k (25, 25), yo, k2, yo, k (15, 15). (116, 116) sts.

Round (98) (largest size only): K (11), yo, k2, yo, k (27), yo, k2, yo, k (27), yo, k2, yo, k (27), yo, k2, yo, k (16). (124) sts.

Round (99) (largest size only): K (12), yo, k2, yo, k (29), yo, k2, yo, k n(29), yo, k2, yo, k (29), yo, k2, yo, k (17). (132) sts.

Rounds 84-89 (90-95, 100-105) (all sizes): K1, p1 rib.

Bind off. Weave in ends.

Eyeballs (make 2)

This pattern is crocheted in spiral. Don't join at the end of a row but continue working.

With the crochet hook and C: Ch4. Join with sl st to form ring.

Round 1: Work 7 sc through ring.
Round 2: Work 2 sc in each sc. 14 sc.
Round 3: Work 14 sc.
Round 4: Work 14 sc.

End with sl st in next st to join.
Fasten off, leaving a tail long enough for sewing.

Pupils (make 2)

With the crochet hook and D: Ch4. Join with sl st to form ring.

Round 1: Work 7 sc through ring.
Fasten off, leaving a tail long enough for sewing.

FINISHING

1 Sew pupil onto the eyeball.
2 With C embroider two small pupils (highlights) in satin stitch.
3 Tuck the loose yarn ends into the dome of the eyeball, and a tiny bit of stuffing if you want.
4 Sew eyes onto the hat.

Teeth

With the crochet hook and B:

Row 1: With right side facing, rejoin yarn at end of sts cast on under chin. Work 1 sc into each of the 7 cast on sts, then work 1 sc into each of the 57 (61, 65) sts around the face opening; end with sl st in first st to join. 64 (68, 72) sc.
Fasten off. Weave in ends.

Row 2: with right side facing rejoin B into row 1 level with the first small fin, and begin to make teeth:
1 sl st, ch4, 1 sl st in 2nd ch from hook, 1 sc in 3rd ch from hook, 1 hdc in 4th ch from hook, skip next sc of row 1, rep. from * to * until you are level with second small fin; end with sl st into next sc. Refer to the photograph for guidance.
Fasten off. Weave in ends.

RIGHT MITTEN

Cuff

Using US 0 (2mm) double-pointed needles, cast on 22 (24, 26) sts and divide evenly among 3 needles. Join to work in the round, being careful not to twist. Place a marker at the beginning of the round.
Rounds 1-10 (1-12, 1-14): Work in k1, p1 rib

Thumb gusset

Switch to US 3 (3.25mm) needles to work rest of mitten.
Round 1: M1L, knit to end of round. 23 (25, 27) sts.
Round 2: Knit.
Round 3: M1L, k1, M1R, k15 (16, 17), yo, k1, yo, k4 (5, 6). 27 (29, 31) sts.
Round 4: K21 (22, 23), yo, k1, yo, k5 (6, 7). 29 (31, 33) sts.
Round 5: M1L, k3, M1R, k17 (18, 19), yo, k1, yo, k6 (7, 8). 33 (35, 37) sts.
Round 6: K25 (26, 27), yo, k1, yo, k7 (8, 9). 35 (37, 39) sts.
Round 7: M1L, k5, M1R, k19 (20, 21), yo, k1, yo, k8 (9, 10). 39 (41, 43) sts.
Round 8: K29 (30, 31), yo, k1, yo, k9 (10, 11). 41 (43, 45) sts.
Round (9, 9) (two larger sizes only): M1L, k7 (7), M1R, k(22)(23), yo, k1, yo, k(11)(12). (47, 49) sts.
Round 9 (10, 10): Place 7 (9, 9) thumb stitches on waste yarn. Rejoin to work hand stitches in the round (34 (38, 40) sts), k23 (25, 26), yo, k1, yo, k10 (12, 13). 36 (40, 42) sts.
Close fin (see page 139 for diagrams)
Round 10 (11, 11): K17 (18, 19), sl next 7 (8, 8) sts, fold right-hand and left-hand needles parallel to each other with wrong sides facing and points facing to the right (right needle is at the back), slip next st onto a crochet hook; it will be the 25th (27th, 28th) st in row.
Insert crochet hook into 24th (26th, 27th) st (from the right needle) and pull this through the loop on hook. Continue in this way:
**pull next st from the left needle through st on hook,
pull next st from right needle through st on hook, **
rep. from ** to ** until the last slipped st on the right needle has been pulled through the next st on the left needle, pull next st from the left needle through st on hook, slip this st back onto the left needle, unfold needles and hold normally, k5 (6, 7). 22 (24, 26) sts.
Rounds 11-22 (12-26, 12-28): Knit.
Closing up the top
Round 23 (27, 29): K2tog to end of round. 11 (12, 13) sts. If you are decreasing and get to the end of the round with only one stitch left, just knit it.
Round 24 (28, 30): Knit. 11 (12, 13) sts.
Round 25 (29, 31): K2tog to end of round. (If

you get to the end of the round with only one stitch left, knit it). 6 (6, 7) sts.
Cut a tail long enough to weave in. Pull through all stitches and remove them from the needle. Pull the tail tightly and secure. Weave in ends.

Thumb

Place 7 (9, 9) stitches from waste yarn onto needles. Rejoin yarn and pick up one extra stitch in the corner where the mitten meets the gusset. 8 (10, 10) sts. Place a marker at the beginning of the round.
Rounds 1-6 (6, 8): Knit.
Round 7 (7, 9): K2tog to end of round. 4 (5, 5) sts.
Finish as for mitten Closing up the top.

LEFT MITTEN

Cuff

Using US 0 (2mm) double-pointed needles, cast on 22 (24, 26) sts and divide evenly among 3 needles. Join to work in the round, being careful not to twist.
Rounds 1-10 (1-12, 1-14): Work in k1, p1 rib.

Thumb gusset

Switch to US 3 (3.25mm) needles to work rest of mitten.
Round 1: M1L, knit to end of round. 23 (25, 27) sts.
Round 2: Knit.
Round 3: M1L, k1, M1R, k4 (5, 6), yo, k1, yo, k15 (16, 17). 27 (29, 31) sts.
Round 4: K10 (11, 12), yo, k1, yo, k16 (17, 18). 29 (31, 33) sts.
Round 5: M1L, k3, M1R, k6 (7, 8), yo, k1, yo, k17 (18, 19). 33 (35, 37) sts.
Round 6: K14 (15, 16), yo, k1, yo, k18 (19, 20). 35 (37, 39) sts.
Round 7: M1L, k5, M1R, k8 (9, 10), yo, k1, yo, k19 (20, 21). 39 (41, 43) sts.
Round 8: K18 (19, 20), yo, k1, yo, k20 (21, 22). 41 (43, 45) sts.
Round (9, 9)(two larger sizes only): M1L, k7 (7), M1R, k(11)(12), yo, k1, yo, k(22)(23). (47, 49) sts.
Round 9 (10, 10): Place 7 (9, 9) thumb stitches on waste yarn. Rejoin to work hand stitches in the round (= 34 (38, 40) sts), k12 (14, 15), yo, k1, yo, k1 (23, 24). 36 (40, 42) sts.
Close fin
Round 10 (11, 11): K6 (7, 8), sl7 (8, 8), fold right-hand and left-hand needles parallel to each other with wrong sides facing and points facing to the right (right needle is at the back), slip next st onto a crochet hook; it will be the 14th (16th, 17th) st in row.
Insert crochet hook into 13th (15th, 16th) st (from

the right needle) and pull this through the loop on hook. Continue in this way:
**pull next st from the left needle through st on hook,
pull next st from right needle through st on hook, **
rep. from ** to ** until the last slipped st on the right needle has been pulled through the next st on the left needle, pull next st from the left needle through st on hook, slip this st back onto the left needle, unfold needles and hold normally, k16 (17, 18). 22 (24, 26) sts.
Rounds 11-22 (12-26, 12-28): Knit.
Closing up the top
Round 23 (27, 29): If you are decreasing and get to the end of the round with only one stitch left, just knit it. K2tog to end of round. 11 (12, 13) sts.
Round 24 (28, 30): Knit.
Round 25 (29, 31): K2tog to end of round. (If you get to the end of the round with only one stitch left, knit it). 6 (6, 7) sts.
Finish as for right mitten Closing up the top.

Thumb

Place 7 (9, 9) stitches from waste yarn onto needles. Rejoin yarn and pick up one extra stitch in the corner where the mitten meets the gusset

Place a marker at the beginning of the round. 8 (10, 10) sts.
Rounds 1-6 (6, 8): Knit.
Round 7 (7, 9): K2tog to end of round. 4 (5, 5) sts.
Finish as for right mitten Closing up the top.

Eyes (make 4):

With 3mm crochet hook and B: Ch3. Join with sl st to form ring.
Round 1: Work 7 sc through ring; end with sl st in next st to join.
Fasten off, leaving a tail long enough for sewing.

Pupils (make 4):

With D, embroider two pupils in satin stitch.
With B, embroider two small highlights in satin stitch.

FINISHING

1 Sew eyes onto the mittens.
2 With B embroider the teeth in back stitch.
3 Weave in ends.

Turn over the mitten to see the shark's sharp teeth!

furry fox

The hat, mittens, and scarf all have little foxy faces, and the scarf even has a fox tail! A knitted strap and crocheted button ensure the hat stays on securely.

HAT, MITTENS, AND SCARF
LEVEL: advanced
SIZES
6-12 months (12-24 months, 2-3 years)
Finished measurements
From "cheek to cheek" around the hat:
14 (14½, 15)in. (36 [37, 38]cm)
Mitten circumference: 5½ (6, 6½)in.
(13.75 [15, 16.25]cm)
Mitten length: 5½ (6½, 7)in.
(14 [16.5, 18]cm)
Scarf length: 33½in. (85cm)
Scarf width: 4½in. (11.5cm)
MATERIALS
HAT
Main yarn:
Color A: 1 x 3oz (85g) ball (135yd/123m)
Lion Brand Jiffy Yarn,
100% acrylic, Paprika
Small amounts:
Color B: Lion Brand Jiffy Yarn,
100% acrylic, White
Color C: Lion Brand Jiffy Yarn,
100% acrylic, Black
Needles:
• 1 pair of US 3 (3.25mm) needles
• 4 x US 3 (3.25mm) double-pointed
needles
• Stitch marker
• US C-2 (2.75mm) crochet hook
• Yarn needle
• Small amount of toy stuffing

MITTENS
Main yarn:
Color A: 1 x 3oz (85g) ball (135yd/123m)
Lion Brand Jiffy Yarn, 100% acrylic, Paprika
Small amounts:
Color B: Lion Brand Jiffy Yarn, 100% acrylic,
White
Color C: Lion Brand Jiffy Yarn, 100% acrylic,
Black
Needles:
• 4 x US 0 (2mm) double-pointed needles
• 4 x US 3 (3.25mm) double-pointed needles
• Yarn needle
SCARF
Main yarn:
Color A: 1 x 3oz (85g) ball (135yd/123m) Lion
Brand Jiffy Yarn, 100% acrylic, Paprika
Small amounts:
Color B: Lion Brand Jiffy Yarn, 100% acrylic,
White
Color C: Lion Brand Jiffy Yarn, 100% acrylic,
Black
Needles:
• 4 x US 3 (3.25mm) double-pointed needles
• Stitch marker
• Yarn needle
GAUGE
16 sts and 25 rows. 4in./10cm square in
stockinette stitch, worked with US 3 (3.25mm)
needles.
19 sts and 28 rows. 4in./10cm square in k1, p1
rib, worked with US 3 (3.25mm) needles

HAT

Using a pair of US 3 (3.25mm) needles and A, cast on 57 (61, 65) sts. Place a stitch marker at the beginning of the row.
Rows 1-6 (6, 6): K1, p1 rib.
Row 7: Knit.
Row 8: K6 (6, 6), p45 (49, 53), k6 (6, 6).
Rep. rows 7 and 8 to row 30 (30, 32).
Row 31 (31, 33): K18 (19, 21), k2tog, k17 (19, 19), k2tog, turn. 55 (59, 63) sts.
Row 32 (32, 34): Sl, p17 (19, 19), p2tog, turn. 54 (58, 62) sts.
Row 33 (33, 35): Sl, k17 (19, 19), k2tog, turn. 53 (57, 61) sts.
Rep. rows 32 (32, 34) and 33 (33, 35) to row 54 (58, 64). 32 (32, 32) sts.
Row 55 (59, 65): Sl, *p1, k1* rep. from * to * 8 (9, 9) times, p1, k2tog, turn. 31 (31, 31) sts.
Row 56 (60, 66): Sl, *k1, p1* rep. from * to * 8 (9, 9) times, k1, p2tog, turn. 30 (30, 30) sts.
Rep. rows 55 (59, 65) and 56 (60, 66) to row 66 (68, 74). 20 (22, 22) sts.
Cut yarn, leaving a long enough tail to weave in. Leave 20 (22, 22) sts on the needle.

Fastening

Rejoin the yarn at marker, push the crochet hook through at the marker from front to back and ch 15.
1 hdc in 5th ch from hook, 1 hdc in next ch, ch2, skip 2 ch, 1 hdc in each of next 6 ch, with right side facing insert hook into edge of rib row 3 and work 1 sc, work a further 14 (14, 15) sc along bottom edge of hat (approximately in each

The strap is soft and comfortable to wear under the chin.

Furry fox hat worn with the scarf for extra warmth.

Follow this photo to position the ears, nose, and eyes.

alternate row) to sts held on needle, taking the sts off the needle one at a time work 1sc into each of the 20 (22, 22) sts, work a further 15 (15, 16) sc along bottom edge of hat (approximately in each alternate row) to front edge.
Fasten off. Weave in ends.

Ears (make 2)

With US 3 (3.25mm) double-pointed needles and A, cast on 20 sts and divide evenly among 3 needles. Join to work in the round, being careful not to twist. Place a marker at the beginning of the round.
Rounds 1–2: Knit.
Round 3: K2tog, k6, *k2tog* twice, k6, k2tog. 16 sts.
Round 4: Knit.
Round 5: K2tog, k4, *k2tog* twice, k4, k2tog. 12 sts.
Round 6: Knit.
Round 7: k2tog, k2, *k2tog* twice, k2, k2tog. 8 sts.
Switch to C.
Round 8: Knit.
Round 9: K2tog 4 times. 4 sts.
Round 10: Knit.
Cut a tail long enough for sewing the ears in place. Pull it through all the stitches and remove them from the needles. Pull the tail tightly and secure.

Inner ear (make 2)

With a pair of US 3 (3.25mm) needles and B, cast on 6 sts, leaving an 8in./20cm tail for sewing the inner parts of the ear in place.
Row 1: Knit.

Row 2: Purl.
Row 3: K2tog, k2, k2tog. 4 sts.
Row 4: Purl.
Row 5: K2tog twice. 2 sts.
Cut a 4in./10cm tail and pull it through 2 stitches. Remove them from the needles. Pull the tail tightly and secure.

Eyes (make 2)

With the crochet hook and C: Ch4. Join with sl st to form a ring.
Round 1: 7sc through ring.
End with sl st in next st to join.
Fasten off, leaving a tail long enough for sewing.

Nose

This pattern is crocheted in spiral. Don't join at the end of a row but continue working.
With the crochet hook and B: Ch4. Join with sl st to form a ring.
Round 1: 7sc through ring.
Round 2: 2sc in each sc. 14sc.
Rounds 3–4: 14sc.
Switch to A.
Rounds 5–6: 14sc.
End with sl st in next st to join.
Fasten off, leaving a tail long enough for sewing.

Nose tip

With the crochet hook and C: Ch4. Join with sl st to form a ring.
Round 1: 6sc through ring.
Round 2: 6sc in each sc in each sc.
End with sl st in next st to join.
Fasten off, leaving a tail long enough for sewing.

Button

With the crochet hook and C: Ch3. Join with sl st to form a ring.
Round 1: 5sc through ring.
End with sl st in next st to join, leaving an 8in./20cm tail for sewing the button in place. Using a yarn needle or crochet hook, pull the tail through all 5 stitches, pull tightly and secure. Make a strong knot.

FINISHING

1 Sew inner parts of the ear onto the ears.
2 Sew the ears onto the hat.
3 Sew the eyes onto the hat.
4 With B embroider two small pupils (highlights) on eyes in satin stitch.
5 With C embroider the eyelashes in satin stitch.
6 Sew the nose tip onto the nose.
7 Tuck the loose yarn ends into the nose, and add a tiny bit of stuffing if you want.
8 Sew the nose onto the hat.
9 Sew the button onto the hat.
10 Weave in ends.

LEFT MITTEN

Cuff

Using US 0 (2mm) double-pointed needles and A, cast on 22 (24, 26) sts and divide evenly among 3 needles. Join to work in the round, being careful not to twist. Place a marker at the beginning of the round.

Rounds 1-10 (1-12, 1-14): Work in k1, p1 rib.

Thumb gusset

Switch to US 3 (3.25mm) double-pointed needles to work rest of mitten.

Round 1: M1R, knit to end of round. 23 (25, 27) sts.
Round 2: Knit.
Round 3: M1R, k1, M1L, knit to end of round. 25 (27, 29) sts.
Round 4: Knit.
Round 5: M1R, k3, M1L, knit to end of round. 27 (29, 31) sts.
Round 6: Knit.
Round 7: M1R, k5, M1L, knit to end of round. 29 (31, 33) sts.
Round 8: Knit.
Round (9, 9) (two larger sizes only): M1R, k7, M1L, knit to end of round. (33, 35) sts.
Round 9 (10, 10): K1, place 7 (9, 9) thumb stitches on waste yarn and rejoin to work hand stitches in the round, k21 (23, 25). 22 (24, 26) sts.
Rounds 10-11 (11-12, 11-14): Knit.

Shape ears

Round 12 (13, 15): K3 (3, 4), yo, k1, yo, k4 (4, 4), yo, k1, yo, k13 (15, 16). 26 (28, 30) sts.

Round 13 (14, 16): K4 (4, 5), yo, k1, yo, k6 (6, 6), yo, k1, yo, k14 (16, 17). 30 (32, 34) sts.
Round 14 (15, 17): K5 (5, 6), yo, k1, yo, k8 (8, 8), yo, k1, yo, k15 (17, 18). 34 (36, 38) sts.
Round 15 (16, 18): K6 (6, 7), yo, k1, yo, k10 (10, 10), yo, k1, yo, k16 (18, 19). 38 (40, 42) sts.
Round 16 (17, 19): K7 (7, 8), yo, k1, yo, k12 (12, 12), yo, k1, yo, k17 (19, 20). 42 (44, 46) sts.
Round 17 (18, 20): K8 (8, 9), yo, k1, yo, k14 (14, 14), yo, k1, yo, k18 (20, 21). 46 (48, 50) sts.
Round (19, 21): K (9, 10), yo, k1, yo, k (16, 16), yo, k1, yo, k (21, 22). (52, 54) sts.

Bind off ears

Close ears (see page 139 for diagrams)
Round 18 (20, 22): K3 (3, 4), slip next 6 (7, 7) sts, fold right and left needles parallel to each other with wrong sides facing and points facing to the right (right needle is at the back), slip next st onto a crochet hook; it will be 10th (11th, 12th) st in row.
Insert crochet hook into 9th (10th, 11th) st (from the right needle) and pull this through the loop on hook. Continue in this way:
**pull next st from the left needle through st on hook,
pull next st from the right needle through st on hook,**
rep. from ** to ** until the last slipped st on the right needle has been pulled through the next st on the left needle, pull next st from the left needle through st on hook, slip this st back onto the left needle, unfold needles and hold normally, k4 (4, 4), sl next 6 (7, 7) sts. Repeat the same way as the first ear until the last

slipped st on the right needle has been pulled through the next st on the left needle, pull next st from the left needle through st on hook, slip this st back onto the left needle, unfold needles and hold normally, k13 (15, 16). 22 (24, 26) sts.
Rounds 19-20 (21-23, 23-25): Knit.
Switch to B.
Rounds 21-22 (24-26, 26-28): Knit.
Closing up the top
Round 23 (27, 29): K2tog to end of round. 11 (12, 13) sts.
Round 24 (28, 30): Knit.
Round 25 (29, 31): K2tog to end of round. (If you get to the end of the round with only one stitch left, knit it.) 6 (6, 7) sts.
Cut a tail long enough to weave in. Pull it through all the stitches and remove them from the needles. Pull the tail tightly and secure. Weave in ends.

Thumb

Place 7 (9, 9) stitches from waste yarn onto US 3 (3.25mm) double-pointed needles. Rejoin yarn and pick up one extra stitch in the corner where the mitten meets the gusset. Place a marker at the beginning of the round. 8 (10, 10) sts.
Rounds 1-6 (1-6, 1-8): Knit.
Round 7 (7, 9): K2tog to end of round. 4 (5, 5) sts.
Finish as for mitten Closing up the top.

Here you can see where to embroider the eyes and nose.

RIGHT MITTEN

Cuff

Using US 0 (2mm) double-pointed needles and A, cast on 22 (24, 26) sts and divide evenly among 3 needles. Join to work in the round, being careful not to twist. Place a marker at the beginning of the round.

Rounds 1–10 (1–12, 1–14): Work in k1, p1 rib.

Thumb gusset

Switch to US 3 (3.25mm) double-pointed needles to work rest of mitten.

Round 1: M1R, knit to end of round. 23 (25, 27) sts.

Round 2: Knit.

Round 3: M1R, k1, M1L, knit to end of round. 25 (27, 29) sts.

Round 4: Knit.

Round 5: M1R, k3, M1L, knit to end of round. 27 (29, 31) sts.

Round 6: Knit.

Round 7: M1R, k5, M1L, knit to end of round. 29 (31, 33) sts.

Round 8: Knit.

Round (9, 9) (two larger sizes only): M1R, k7, M1L, knit to end of round. (33, 35) sts.

Round 9 (10, 10): K1, place 7 (9, 9) thumb stitches on waste yarn and rejoin to work hand stitches in the round, k21 (23, 25). 22 (24, 26) sts.

Rounds 10–11 (11–12, 11–14): Knit.

Shape ears

Round 12 (13, 15): K13 (15, 16), yo, k1, yo, k4 (4, 4), yo, k1, yo, k3 (3, 4). 26 (28, 30) sts.

Round 13 (14, 16): K14 (16, 17), yo, k1, yo, k6 (6, 6), yo, k1, yo, k4 (4, 5). 30 (32, 34) sts.

Round 14 (15, 17): K15 (17, 18), yo, k1, yo, k8 (8, 8), yo, k1, yo, k5 (5, 6). 34 (36, 38) sts.

Round 15 (16, 18): K16 (18, 19), yo, k1, yo, k10 (10, 10), yo, k1, yo, k6 (6, 7). 38 (40, 42) sts.

Round 16 (17, 19): K17 (19, 20), yo, k1, yo, k12 (12, 12), yo, k1, yo, k7 (7, 8). 42 (44, 46) sts.

Round 17 (18, 20): K18 (20, 21), yo, k1, yo, k14 (14, 14), yo, k1, yo, k8 (8, 9). 46 (48, 50) sts.

Round (19, 21): K (21, 22), yo, k1, yo, k (16, 16), yo, k1, yo, k (9, 10). (52, 54) sts.

Close ears

Round 18 (20, 22): K13 (15, 16), slip next 6 (7, 7) sts, fold right and left needles parallel to each other with wrong sides facing and points facing to the right (right needle is at the back), slip next st onto a crochet hook; it will be 20th (23rd, 24th) st in row.

Insert crochet hook into 19th (22nd, 23rd) st (from the right needle) and pull this through the loop on hook. Continue in this way:

pull next st from the left needle through st on hook, pull next st from the right needle through st on hook, rep. from ** to ** until the last slipped st on the right needle has been pulled through the next st on the left needle, pull next st from the left needle through st on hook, slip this st back onto the left needle, unfold needles and hold normally, k4 (4, 4), sl next 6 (7, 7) sts. Repeat the same way as the first ear until the last slipped st on the right needle has been pulled through the next st on the left needle, pull next st from the left needle through st on hook, slip this st back onto the left needle, unfold needles and hold normally, k3 (3, 4). 22 (24, 26) sts.

Rounds 19–20 (21–23, 23–25): Knit.

Switch to B.

Rounds 21–22 (24–26, 26–28): Knit.

Closing up the top

Round 23 (27, 29): K2tog to end of round. 11 (12, 13) sts.

Round 24 (28, 30): Knit.

Round 25 (29, 31): K2tog to end of round. (If you get to the end of the round with only one stitch left, knit it.) 6 (6, 7) sts.

Finish as for left mitten Closing up the top.

Thumb

Place 7 (9, 9) stitches from waste yarn onto US 3 (3.25mm) double-pointed needles. Rejoin yarn and pick up one extra stitch in the corner where the mitten meets the gusset. Place a marker at the beginning of the round. 8 (10, 10) sts.

Rounds 1–6 (1–6, 1–8): Knit.

Round 7 (7, 9): K2tog to end of round. 4 (5, 5) sts.

Finish as for left mitten Closing up the top.

FINISHING

1 Using C, embroider the eyes and nose in satin stitch.

2 Weave in ends.

Once you have mastered fox mittens, why not make several pairs as gifts?

SCARF

Using US 3 (3.25mm) double-pointed needles and B, cast on 3 sts and divide evenly among 3 needles. Join to work in the round, being careful not to twist. Place a marker at the beginning of the round. The scarf starts from the fox's tail.

Rounds 1-2: K3.
Round 3: *K1, M1* 3 times. 6 sts.
Round 4: Knit.
Round 5: *K1, M1, k1* 3 times. 9 sts.
Round 6: Knit.
Round 7: *K1, M1, k2* 3 times. 12 sts.
Round 8: Knit
Round 9: *K1, M1, k3* 3 times. 15 sts.
Round 10: Knit.
Round 11: *K1, M1, k4* 3 times. 18 sts.
Round 12: Knit.
Round 13: *K1, M1, k5* 3 times. 21 sts.
Round 14: Knit.
Round 15: *K1, M1, k6* 3 times. 24 sts.
Round 16: Knit.
Round 17: *K1, M1, k7* 3 times. 27 sts.
Round 18: Knit.
Round 19: *K1, M1, k8* 3 times. 30 sts.
Round 20: Knit.
Switch to A.
Round 21: *K1, M1, k9* 3 times. 33 sts.
Round 22: Knit.
Round 23: *K1, M1, k10* 3 times. 36 sts.
Round 24: Knit.
Round 25: *K1, M1, k11* 3 times. 39 sts.
Round 26: Knit.
Rounds 27-44: Knit.
Round 45: *K1, p1* 18 times, k1, p2tog. 38 sts.
Rounds 46-50: K1, p1 rib.
Round 51: K2, place next 5 sts onto waste yarn, cast on 5 sts, k5, place next 5 sts onto waste yarn, cast on 5 sts, k21. 38 sts.
Rounds 52-132: Knit.
Round 133: Rep. round 51.
Rounds 134-143: Knit.
Round 144: *K2tog, p1, k1, p1* 7 times, k2tog, p1. 30 sts.
Rounds 145-149: K1, p1 rib.
Rounds 150-160: Knit.
Round 161: K19, yo, k1, yo, k5, yo, k1, yo, k4. 34 sts.
Round 162: K20, yo, k1, yo, k7, yo, k1, yo, k5. 38 sts.
Round 163: K21, yo, k1, yo, k9, yo, k1, yo, k6. 42 sts.
Round 164: K22, yo, k1, yo, k11, yo, k1, yo, k7. 46 sts.
Round 165: K23, yo, k1, yo, k13, yo, k1, yo, k8. 50 sts.
Round 166: K24, yo, k1, yo, k15, yo, k1, yo, k9. 54 sts.
Round 167: K25, yo, k1, yo, k17, yo, k1, yo, k10. 58 sts.
Close ears (see page 139 for diagrams)
Round 168: K19, slip next 7 sts, fold right and left needles parallel to each other with wrong sides facing and points facing to the right (right needle is at the back), slip next st onto a crochet hook; it will be 27th st in row.
Insert crochet hook into 26th st (from the right needle) and pull this through the loop on hook.

This gorgeous scarf is truly original with paws as well as a foxy face and luxurious tail.

Continue in this way:
**pull next st from the left needle through st on hook,
pull next st from the right needle through st on hook,**
rep. from ** to ** until the last slipped st on the right needle has been pulled through the next st on the left needle, pull next st from the left needle through st on hook, slip this st back onto the left needle, unfold needles and hold normally, k5, sl next 7 sts. Repeat the same way as the first ear until the last slipped st on the right needle has been pulled through the next st on the left needle, pull next st from the left needle through st on hook, slip this st back onto the left needle, unfold needles and hold normally, k4. 30 sts.
Rounds 169-175: Knit.
Switch to B.
Round 176: Knit.
Round 177: K2tog to end of round. 15 sts.
Round 178: Knit.
Round 179: K1, K2tog to end of round. 8 sts.

Round 180: Knit.
Round 181: K2tog to end of round. 4 sts.
Round 182: Knit.
Cut a tail long enough to weave in. Pull it through all 4 stitches and remove them from the needles. Pull the tail tightly and secure.

Paws (make 4)

Place 5 stitches from waste yarn onto US 3 (3.25mm) double-pointed needles, pick up 5 sts across the 5 cast-on sts. 10 sts.
Rounds 1-30: Knit.
Switch to C.
Rounds 31-39: Knit.
Round 40: K2tog to end of round. 5 sts.
Round 41: Knit.
Round 42: K1, k2tog to end of round. 3 sts.
Finish off as for main part of Scarf.

FINISHING

1 Embroider the eyes and nose in satin stitch.
2 Weave in ends.

funky frog

The eyeballs, crocheted in spiral, and the wide, pink mouth give the frog its zany, offbeat look. The details are repeated on the mittens to complete this lovable set.

COVERALL HAT AND MITTENS
LEVEL: advanced
SIZES
6-12 months (12-24 months, 2-3 years)
Finished measurements
From "cheek to cheek" around the hat:
14 (14½, 15)in. (36 [37, 38]cm)
Mitten circumference: 5½ (6, 6½)in. (13.75 [15, 16.25]cm)
Mitten length: 5½ (6½, 7)in. (14 [16.5, 18]cm)
MATERIALS
HAT
Main yarn:
Color A: 1 x 3oz (85g) ball (135yd/123m) Lion Brand Jiffy Yarn, 100% acrylic, Apple Green
Small amounts:
Color B: Lion Brand Jiffy Yarn, 100% acrylic, White
Color C: Lion Brand Jiffy Yarn, 100% acrylic, Blossom
Color D: Lion Brand Jiffy Yarn, 100% acrylic, Black
Needles:
• 1 pair of US 3 (3.25mm) needles
• US 3 (3.25mm) circular needles
• Stitch marker

• US C-2 (2.75mm) crochet hook
• Yarn needle
• Small amount of toy stuffing
MITTENS
Main yarn:
Color A: 1 x 3oz (85g) ball (135yd/123m) Lion Brand Jiffy Yarn, 100% acrylic, Apple Green
Small amounts:
Color B: Lion Brand Jiffy Yarn, 100% acrylic, White
Color C: Lion Brand Jiffy Yarn, 100% acrylic, Blossom
Color D: Lion Brand Jiffy Yarn, 100% acrylic, Black
Needles:
• 4 x US 0 (2mm) double-pointed needles
• 4 x US 3 (3.25mm) double-pointed needles
• US C-2 (2.75mm) crochet hook
• Yarn needle
GAUGE
16 sts and 25 rows. 4in./10cm square in stockinette stitch worked with US 3 (3.25mm) needles.
19 sts and 28 rows. 4in./10cm square in k1, p1 rib worked with US 3 (3.25mm) needles.

HAT

Using a pair of US 3 (3.25mm) needles and A, cast on 57 (61, 65) sts.
Rows 1-6 (6, 6): K1, p1 rib.
Rows 7- 30 (30, 32): Work in stockinette stitch, starting with a k row.
Row 31 (31, 33): K18 (19, 21), k2tog, k17 (19, 19), k2tog, turn. 55 (59, 63) sts.
Row 32 (32, 34): Sl, p17 (19, 19), p2tog, turn. 54 (58, 62) sts.
Row 33 (33, 35): Sl, k17 (19, 19), k2tog, turn. 53 (57, 61) sts.
Rep. rows 32 (32, 34) and 33 (33, 35) to row 54 (56, 62). 32 (34, 34) sts.
Row 55 (57, 63): Sl, *p1, k1* rep. from * to * 8 (9, 9) times, p1, k2tog, turn. 31 (33, 33) sts.
Row 56 (58, 64): Sl, *k1, p1* rep. from * to * 8 (9, 9) times, k1, p2tog, turn. 30 (32, 32) sts.
Rep. rows 55 (57, 63) and 56 (58, 64) to row 66 (68, 74). 20 (22, 22) sts.

Neck ruff

Switch to US 3 (3.25mm) circular needles. Place a marker at the beginning of the round.
Round 67 (69, 75): Sl, *p1, k1* rep. from * to * 8 (9, 9) times, p1, k2tog, pick up 13 (12, 12) sts on one side of the hat, cast on 7 (7, 7) sts, join to work in the round, being careful not to twist, pick up 13 (12, 12) sts on the other side of the hat. 52 (52, 52) sts.
Rounds 68-77 (70-81, 76-89): K1, p1 rib.
Round 78 (82, 90): K2 (3, 3), yo, k2, yo, k11 (11, 11), yo, k2, yo, k11 (11, 11), yo, k2, yo, k11 (11, 11), yo, k2, yo, k9 (8, 8). 60 (60, 60) sts.
Round 79 (83, 91): K3 (4, 4), yo, k2, yo, k13 (13, 13), yo, k2, yo, k13 (13, 13), yo, k2, yo, k13 (13, 13), yo, k2, yo, k10 (9, 9). 68 (68, 68) sts.
Round 80 (84, 92): K4 (5, 5), yo, k2, yo, k15 (15, 15), yo, k2, yo, k15 (15, 15), yo, k2, yo, k15 (15, 15), yo, k2, yo, k11 (10, 10). 76 (76, 76) sts.
Round 81 (85, 93): K5 (6, 6), yo, k2, yo, k17 (17, 17), yo, k2, yo, k17 (17, 17), yo, k2, yo, k17 (17, 17), yo, k2, yo, k12 (11, 11). 84 (84, 84) sts.
Round 82 (86, 94): K6 (7, 7), yo, k2, yo, k19 (19, 19), yo, k2, yo, k19 (19, 19), yo, k2, yo, k19 (19, 19), yo, k2, yo, k13 (12, 12). 92 (92, 92) sts.
Round 83 (87, 95): K7 (8, 8), yo, k2, yo, k21 (21, 21), yo, k2, yo, k21 (21, 21), yo, k2, yo, k21 (21, 21), yo, k2, yo, k14 (13, 13). 100 (100, 100) sts.
Round (88, 96) (two larger sizes only): K (9, 9), yo, k2, yo, k (23, 23), yo, k2, yo, k (23, 23), yo, k2, yo, k (23, 23), yo, k2, yo, k (14, 14). (108, 108) sts.

Make sure your funky frog has a wide embroidered grin on his face.

Round (89, 97) (two larger sizes only): K (10, 10), yo, k2, yo, k (25, 25), yo, k2, yo, k (25, 25), yo, k2, yo, k (25, 25), yo, k2, yo, k (15, 15). (116, 116) sts.

Round (98) (largest size only): K (11), yo, k2, yo, k (27), yo, k2, yo, k (27), yo, k2, yo, k (27), yo, k2, yo, k (16). (124) sts.

Round (99) (largest size only): K (12), yo, k2, yo, k (29), yo, k2, yo, k (29), yo, k2, yo, k (29), yo, k2, yo, k (17). (132) sts.

Rounds 84-89 (90-95, 100-105) (all sizes): K1, p1 rib.
Bind off. Weave in ends.

Eyes

Eye-socket (make 2)
Using a pair of US 3 (3.25mm) needles and A, cast on 25 sts, leaving an 8in./20cm tail for sewing the eye-sockets in place.

Rows 1-5: K1, p1 rib.
Cut tail long enough to weave in. Pull through all 25 stitches. Remove them from needle. Pull the tail tightly and secure. Make a strong knot. Sew the side seam.

Eyeballs (make 2)
This pattern is crocheted in spiral. Don't join at the end of a row but continue working.

With a US C-2 (2.75mm) crochet hook and B, ch4. Join with sl st to form ring.
Round 1: 7sc through ring.
Round 2: 2sc in each sc. 14 sc.
Round 3: 14sc.
Round 4: 14sc.
End with sl st in next st to join.
Fasten off, leaving a tail long enough for sewing.

Pupils (make 2)
With a US C-2 (2.75mm) crochet hook and D, ch4. Join with sl st to form ring.
Round 1: 7sc through ring.
End with sl st in next st to join.
Fasten off, leaving a tail long enough for sewing.

FINISHING
1 Sew pupil onto the eyeball.
2 With B embroider two small pupils (highlights) in satin stitch.
3 Tuck the loose yarn ends into the dome of the eyeball, and a tiny bit of stuffing if you want.
4 Sew eyeballs into the eye-sockets.
5 Sew eyes onto the hat.
6 With C embroider the smiling mouth using backstitch.
7 Weave in ends.

The funky frog looks attractive from the back with the pattern on the back of the eyes.

MITTENS

(make 2)

Cuff

Using US 0 (2mm) double-pointed needles and A, cast on 22 (24, 26) sts and divide evenly among 3 needles. Join to work in the round, being careful not to twist. Place a marker at the beginning of the round.
Rounds 1-10 (1-12, 1-14): Work in k1, p1 rib.

Thumb gusset

Switch to US 3 (3.25mm) double-pointed needles to work rest of mitten.
Round 1: M1R, knit to end of round. 23 (25, 27) sts.
Round 2: Knit.
Round 3: M1R, k1, M1L, knit to end of round. 25 (27, 29) sts.
Round 4: Knit.
Round 5: M1R, k3, M1L, knit to end of round. 27 (29, 31) sts.
Round 6: Knit.
Round 7: M1R, k5, M1L, knit to end of round. 29 (31, 33) sts.
Round 8: Knit.
Round (9, 9) (two larger sizes only): M1R, k7, M1L, knit to end of round. (33, 35) sts.
Round 9 (10, 10): K1, place 7 (9, 9) thumb stitches on waste yarn. Rejoin to work hand stitches in the round, k21 (23, 25). 22 (24, 26) sts.
Rounds 10-22 (11-26, 11-28): Knit.

Closing up the top

Round 23 (27, 29): K2tog to end of round. 11 (12, 13) sts.
Round 24 (28, 30): Knit.
Round 25 (29, 31): K2tog to end of round. (If you get to the end of the round with only one stitch left, knit it.) 6 (6, 7) sts.
Cut a tail long enough to weave in. Pull it through all the stitches and remove them from the needles. Pull the tail tightly and secure. Weave in ends.

Thumb

Place 7 (9, 9) stitches from waste yarn onto US 3 (3.25mm) double-pointed needles. Rejoin yarn and pick up one extra stitch in the corner where the mitten meets the gusset. 8 (10, 10) sts.
Rounds 1-6 (1-6, 1-8): Knit.
Round 7 (7, 9): K2tog to end of round. 4 (5, 5) sts.
Finish as for mitten Closing up the top.

Eyeballs and Pupils
(make 4 of each)

Make as for Eyeballs and Pupils on Hat.

FINISHING

1 Sew the eyes onto the mittens.
2 With C embroider the smiling mouth using backstitch.
3 Weave in ends.

Position the eyes on the mittens so that the right mitten mirrors the left.

festive friends

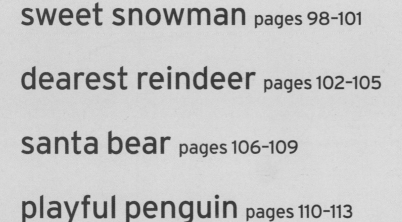

sweet snowman

The snowman hat has red pompoms to keep little ears extra warm, and the stripes on the back match the mittens. As well as making the pompoms, some crochet is needed.

COVERALL HAT AND MITTENS
LEVEL: beginner
SIZES
6-12 months (12-24 months, 2-3 years)
Finished measurements
From "cheek to cheek" around the hat:
14 (14½, 15)in. (36 [37, 38]cm)
Mitten circumference: 5½ (6, 6½)in.
(13.75 [15, 16.25]cm)
Mitten length: 5½ (6½, 7)in. (14 [16.5, 18]cm)
Materials
HAT
Main yarn:
Color A: 1 x 3oz (85g) ball (135yd/123m) Lion Brand Jiffy Yarn, 100% acrylic, White
Small amounts:
Color B: Lion Brand Jiffy Yarn, 100% acrylic, True Red
Color C: Lion Brand Jiffy Yarn, 100% acrylic, Black
Color D: Lion Brand Jiffy Yarn, 100% acrylic, Rust
Needles:
• 1 pair of US 3 (3.25mm) needles
• US 3 (3.25mm) circular needle
• Stitch marker
• US C-2 (2.75mm) crochet hook

• 4 x US 3 (3.25mm) double-pointed needles
• Two circles of cardboard 3in./8cm in diameter or a pompom maker
• Yarn needle
• Small amount of toy stuffing
MITTENS
Main yarn:
Color A: 1 x 3oz (85g) ball (135yd/123m) Lion Brand Jiffy Yarn, 100% acrylic, White
Small amounts:
Color B: Lion Brand Jiffy Yarn, 100% acrylic, True Red
Color C: Lion Brand Jiffy Yarn, 100% acrylic, Black
Color D: Lion Brand Jiffy Yarn, 100% acrylic, Rust
Needles:
• 4 x US 0 (2mm) double-pointed needles
• 4 x US 3 (3.25mm) double-pointed needles
• US C-2 (2.75mm) crochet hook
• Yarn needle
GAUGE
16 sts and 25 rows = 4in./10cm square in stockinette stitch, worked with US 3 (3.25mm) needles.
19 sts and 28 rows = 4in./10cm square in k1, p1 rib, worked with US 3 (3.25mm) needles.

HAT

Using a pair of US 3 (3.25mm) needles and A, cast on 57 (61, 65) sts.
Rows 1-6 (6, 6): K1, p1 rib.
Rows 7- 30 (30, 32): Work in stockinette stitch, starting with a k row.
Row 31 (31, 33): K18 (19, 21), k2tog, k17 (19, 19), k2tog, turn. 55 (59, 63) sts.
Row 32 (32, 34): Sl, p17 (19, 19), p2tog, turn. 54 (58, 62) sts.
Row 33 (33, 35): Sl, k17 (19, 19), k2tog, turn. 53 (57, 61) sts.
Rep. rows 32 (32, 34) and 33 (33, 35) to row 54 (56, 62). 32 (34, 34) sts.
Row 55 (57, 63): Sl, *p1, k1* rep. from * to * 8 (9, 9) times, p1, k2tog, turn. 31 (33, 33) sts.
Row 56 (58, 64): Sl, *k1, p1* rep. from * to * 8 (9, 9) times, k1, p2tog, turn. 30 (32, 32) sts.
Rep. rows 55 (57, 63) and 56 (58, 64) to row 66 (68, 74). 20 (22, 22) sts.

Neck ruff

Switch to a US 3 (3.25mm) circular needle and B. Place a marker at the beginning of the round.
Round 67 (69, 75): Sl, *p1, k1* rep. from * to * 8 (9, 9) times, p1, k2tog, pick up 13 (12, 12) sts on one side of the hat, cast on 7 (7, 7) sts, join to work in the round, being careful not to twist, pick up 13 (12, 12) sts on the other side of the hat. 52 (52, 52) sts.

This set is bound to be a favorite for chilly winter days.

Attach the nose in the center, with the eyes an equal distance either side. The pompoms should be over the child's ears.

Rounds 68-77 (70-81, 76-89): K1, p1 rib in the following stripe pattern:
2 (2, 2) rounds (B),
3 (3, 3) rounds (A),
3 (3, 3) rounds (B),
2 (3, 3) rounds (A),
0 (1, 3) rounds (B).
Switch to A.
Round 78 (82, 90): K2 (3, 3), yo, k2, yo, k11 (11, 11), yo, k2, yo, k11 (11, 11), yo, k2, yo, k11 (11, 11), yo, k2, yo, k9 (8, 8). 60 (60, 60) sts.
Round 79 (83, 91): K3 (4, 4), yo, k2, yo, k13 (13, 13), yo, k2, yo, k13 (13, 13), yo, k2, yo, k13 (13, 13), yo, k2, yo, k10 (9, 9). 68 (68, 68) sts.
Round 80 (84, 92): K4 (5, 5), yo, k2, yo, k15 (15, 15), yo, k2, yo, k15 (15, 15), yo, k2, yo, k15 (15, 15), yo, k2, yo, k11 (10, 10). 76 (76, 76) sts.
Round 81 (85, 93): K5 (6, 6), yo, k2, yo, k17 (17, 17), yo, k2, yo, k17 (17, 17), yo, k2, yo, k17 (17, 17), yo, k2, yo, k12 (11, 11). 84 (84, 84) sts.
Round 82 (86, 94): K6 (7, 7), yo, k2, yo, k19 (19, 19), yo, k2, yo, k19 (19, 19), yo, k2, yo, k19 (19, 19), yo, k2, yo, k13 (12, 12). 92 (92, 92) sts.
Round 83 (87, 95): K7 (8, 8), yo, k2, yo, k21 (21, 21), yo, k2, yo, k21 (21, 21), yo, k2, yo, k21 (21, 21), yo, k2, yo, k14 (13, 13). 100 (100, 100) sts.
Round (88, 96) (two larger sizes only): K (9, 9), yo, k2, yo, k (23, 23), yo, k2, yo, k (23, 23), yo, k2, yo, k (23, 23), yo, k2, yo, k (14, 14). (108, 108) sts.
Round (89, 97) (two larger sizes only): K (10, 10), yo, k2, yo, k (25, 25), yo, k2, yo, k (25, 25), yo, k2, yo, k (25, 25), yo, k2, yo, k (15, 15). (116, 116) sts.

Round (98) (largest size only): K (11), yo, k2, yo, k (27), yo, k2, yo, k (27), yo, k2, yo, k (27), yo, k2, yo, k (16). (124) sts.
Round (99) (largest size only): K (12), yo, k2, yo, k (29), yo, k2, yo, k (29), yo, k2, yo, k (29), yo, k2, yo, k (17). (132) sts.
Rounds 84-89 (90-95, 100-105) (all sizes):
K1, p1 rib.
Bind off. Weave in ends.

Eyes (make 2)

With the crochet hook and C: Ch4. Join with sl st to form ring.
Round 1: 7sc through ring.
End with sl st in next st to join.
Fasten off, leaving a tail long enough for sewing.

Pompoms (make 2 in B)

See page 140 for how to make pompoms or use a pompom maker.

Headband

With the crochet hook and B: Ch44.
1hdc in 3rd ch from hook, 1hdc in each next ch to end.
Fasten off, leaving a tail long enough for sewing.

Nose

With US 3 (3.25mm) double-pointed needles and D, cast on 12 sts. Join to work in the round, being careful not to twist. Place a marker at the beginning of the round.

The striped pattern on the back of the hat matches the mittens.

Rounds 1-2: Knit.
Round 3: *K2, k2tog* 3 times. 9 sts.
Round 4: Knit.
Round 5: *K1, k2tog* 3 times. 6 sts.
Round 6: Knit.
Round 7: K2tog 3 times. 3 sts.
Round 8: Knit.
Cut a tail long enough to weave in. Pull it through all the stitches and remove them from the needles. Pull the tail tightly and secure.

FINISHING
1 Sew the eyes onto the hat.
2 Tuck the loose yarn ends into the nose, and add a tiny bit of stuffing if you want.
3 Sew the nose onto the hat.
4 Sew the headband onto the hat.
5 Sew the pompoms onto the hat.
6 Weave in ends.

MITTENS

(MAKE 2)

Cuff
Using US 0 (2mm) double-pointed needles and B, cast on 22 (24, 26) sts and divide evenly among 3 needles. Join to work in the round, being careful not to twist. Place a marker at the beginning of the round.
Rounds 1-10 (1-12, 1-14): Work in k1, p1 rib in the following stripe pattern:
2 (2, 2) rounds (B),
3 (3, 3) rounds (A),
3 (3, 3) rounds (B),
2 (3, 3) rounds (A),
0 (1, 3) rounds (B).

Thumb gusset
Switch to US 3 (3.25mm) double-pointed needles and A to work rest of mitten.
Round 1: M1R, knit to end of round. 23 (25, 27) sts.
Round 2: Knit.
Round 3: M1R, k1, M1L, knit to end of round. 25 (27, 29) sts.
Round 4: Knit.
Round 5: M1R, k3, M1L, knit to end of round. 27 (29, 31) sts.
Round 6: Knit.
Round 7: M1R, k5, M1L, knit to end of round. 29 (31, 33) sts.
Round 8: Knit.
Round (9, 9) (two larger sizes only): M1R, k7, M1L, knit to end of round. (33, 35) sts.
Round 9 (10, 10): K1, place 7 (9, 9) thumb stitches on waste yarn and rejoin to work hand stitches in the round, k21 (23, 25). 22 (24, 26) sts.
Rounds 10-22 (11-26, 11-28): Knit.

Closing up the top
Round 23 (27, 29): K2tog to end of round. 11 (12, 13) sts.
Round 24 (28, 30): Knit.
Round 25 (29, 31): K2tog to end of round. (If you get to the end of the round with only one stitch left, knit it.) 6 (6, 7) sts.
Cut a tail long enough to weave in. Pull it through all the stitches and remove them from the needles. Pull the tail tightly and secure. Weave in ends.

Thumb
Place 7 (9, 9) stitches from waste yarn onto US 3 (3.25mm) double-pointed needles and A. Rejoin yarn and pick up one extra stitch in the corner where the mitten meets the gusset. Place a marker at the beginning of the round. 8 (10, 10) sts.
Rounds 1-6 (1-6, 1-8): Knit.
Round 7 (7, 9): K2tog to end of round. 4 (5, 5) sts.
Finish as for mitten Closing up the top.

Simple stripes in stockinette stitch make the mittens special.

dearest reindeer

With sweet little horns and red nose, the reindeer hat and its matching mittens are sure to be a winter favorite. Some crocheting is required to make the ears.

COVERALL HAT AND MITTENS
LEVEL: intermediate
SIZES
6-12 months (12-24 months, 2-3 years)
Finished measurements
Hat measurements (lying flat)
From "cheek to cheek" around the hat:
14 (14½, 15)in. (36 [37, 38]cm)
Mitten circumference: 5½ (6, 6½)in.
(13.75 [15, 16.25]cm)
Mitten length: 5½ (6½, 7)in. (14 [16.5, 18]cm)
MATERIALS
HAT
Main yarn:
Color A: 1 x 3oz (85g) ball (135yd/123m) Lion Brand Jiffy Yarn, 100% acrylic, Taupe Mist
Small amounts:
Color B: Lion Brand Jiffy Yarn, 100% acrylic, True Red
Color C: Lion Brand Jiffy Yarn, 100% acrylic, Camel
Color D: Lion Brand Jiffy Yarn, 100% acrylic, Violet
Needles:
• 1 pair of US 3 (3.25mm) needles
• US 3 (3.25mm) circular needle

• 4 x US 0 (2mm) double-pointed needles
• Stitch marker
• US C-2 (2.75mm) crochet hook
• Yarn needle
MITTENS
Main yarn:
Color A: 1 x 3oz (85g) ball (135yd/123m) Lion Brand Jiffy Yarn, 100% acrylic, Taupe Mist
Small amounts:
Color B: Lion Brand Jiffy Yarn, 100% acrylic, True Red
Color C: Lion Brand Jiffy Yarn, 100% acrylic, Camel
Color D: Lion Brand Jiffy Yarn, 100% acrylic, Violet
Needles:
• 4 x US 0 (2mm) double-pointed needles
• 4 x US 3 (3.25mm) double-pointed needles
• US C-2 (2.75mm) crochet hook
• Yarn needle
GAUGE
16 sts and 25 rows = 4in./10cm square in stockinette stitch, worked with US 3 (3.25mm) needles.
19 sts and 28 rows = 4in./10cm square in k1, p1 rib, worked with US 3 (3.25mm) needles.

HAT

Using a pair of US 3 (3.25mm) needles and A, cast on 57 (61, 65) sts.
Rows 1-6 (6, 6): K1, p1 rib.
Rows 7- 30 (30, 32): Work in stockinette stitch, starting with a k row.
Row 31 (31, 33): K18 (19, 21), k2tog, k17 (19, 19), k2tog, turn. 55 (59, 63) sts.
Row 32 (32, 34): Sl, p17 (19, 19), p2tog, turn. 54 (58, 62) sts.
Row 33 (33, 35): Sl, k17 (19, 19), k2tog, turn. 53 (57, 61) sts.
Rep. rows 32 (32, 34) and 33 (33, 35) to row 54 (56, 62). 32 (34, 34) sts.
Row 55 (57, 63): Sl, *p1, k1* rep. from * to * 8 (9, 9) times, p1, k2tog, turn. 31 (33, 33) sts.
Row 56 (58, 64): Sl, *k1, p1* rep. from * to * 8 (9, 9) times; k1, p2tog, turn. 30 (32, 32) sts.
Rep. rows 55 (57, 63) and 56 (58, 64) to row 66 (68, 74). 20 (22, 22) sts.

Neck ruff

Switch to a US 3 (3.25mm) circular needle. Place a marker at the beginning of the round.
Round 67 (69, 75): Sl, *p1, k1* rep. from * to * 8 (9, 9) times, p1, k2tog, pick up 13 (12, 12) sts on one side of the hat, cast on 7 (7, 7) sts, join to work in the round, being careful not to twist, pick up 13 (12, 12) sts on the other side of the hat. 52 (52, 52) sts.
Rounds 68-77 (70-81, 76-89): K1, p1 rib.
Round 78 (82, 90): K2 (3, 3), yo, k2, yo, k11 (11, 11), yo, k2, yo, k11 (11, 11), yo, k2, yo, k11 (11, 11), yo, k2, yo, k9 (8, 8). 60 (60, 60) sts.
Round 79 (83, 91): K3 (4, 4), yo, k2, yo, k13 (13, 13), yo, k2, yo, k13 (13, 13), yo, k2, yo, k13 (13, 13), yo, k2, yo, k10 (9, 9). 68 (68, 68) sts.
Round 80 (84, 92): K4 (5, 5), yo, k2, yo, k15 (15, 15), yo, k2, yo, k15 (15, 15), yo, k2, yo, k15 (15, 15), yo, k2, yo, k11 (10, 10). 76 (76, 76) sts.
Round 81 (85, 93): K5 (6, 6), yo, k2, yo, k17 (17, 17), yo, k2, yo, k17 (17, 17), yo, k2, yo, k17 (17, 17), yo, k2, yo, k12 (11, 11). 84 (84, 84) sts.
Round 82 (86, 94): K6 (7, 7), yo, k2, yo, k19 (19, 19), yo, k2, yo, k19 (19, 19), yo, k2, yo, k19 (19, 19), yo, k2, yo, k13 (12, 12). 92 (92, 92) sts.
Round 83 (87, 95): K7 (8, 8), yo, k2, yo, k21 (21, 21), yo, k2, yo, k21 (21, 21), yo, k2, yo, k21 (21, 21), yo, k2, yo, k14 (13, 13). 100 (100, 100) sts.
Round (88, 96) (two larger sizes only): K (9, 9), yo, k2, yo, k (23, 23), yo, k2, yo, k (23, 23), yo, k2, yo, k (23, 23), yo, k2, yo, k (14, 14). (108, 108) sts.
Round (89, 97) (two larger sizes only): K (10, 10), yo, k2, yo, k (25, 25), yo, k2, yo, k (25, 25), yo, k2, yo, k (25, 25), yo, k2, yo, k (15, 15). (116, 116) sts.

Position the features as shown here, starting with the red nose in the center.

The reindeer design is just as effective when viewed in profile.

Round (98) (largest size only): K (11), yo, k2, yo, k (27), yo, k2, yo, k (27), yo, k2, yo, k (27), yo, k2, yo, k (16). (124) sts.
Round (99) (largest size only): K (12), yo, k2, yo, k (29), yo, k2, yo, k (29), yo, k2, yo, k (29), yo, k2, yo, k (17). (132) sts.
Rounds 84-89 (90-95, 100-105) (all sizes): K1, p1 rib.
Bind off. Weave in ends.

Ears (make 2)
With the crochet hook and A: Ch9.
Row 1: 1dc in 3rd ch from hook, 1dc in each of next 5 sts, 8dc in last ch, (turn work so you are working on bottom of chain), 1dc in each of next 7 ch, turn. 21 dc.
Row 2: Ch1, 1sc in each of next 7 sts, 2sc in each of next 3 sts, (1sc and 1hdc) both in next st, (1hdc and 1sc) both in next st, 2sc in each of next 3 sts, 1sc in each of next 6 sts.
Fasten off, leaving a tail long enough for sewing.

The crocheted nose is sewn just above the edge of the hat.

Antlers (make 2)
With US 0 (2mm) double-pointed needles and C, cast on 8 sts and divide evenly among 3 needles. Join to work in the round, being careful not to twist. Place a marker at the beginning of the round.
Rounds 1-6: Knit.
Shape small horn
Round 7: K1, M1, k7. 9 sts.
Round 8: Knit.
Round 9: K1, M1, k1, M1, k7. 11 sts.
Round 10: Knit.
Round 11: K1, M1, k3, M1, k7. 13 sts.
Round 12: Knit.
Round 13: K1, place next 5 sts on waste yarn and rejoin to work horn stitches in the round, k7. 8 sts.
Rounds 14-18: Knit.
Round 19: K2tog to end of round. 4 sts.
Cut a tail long enough to weave in. Pull it through all the stitches and remove them from the needles. Pull the tail tightly and secure.
Small horn
Place 5 stitches from waste yarn onto US 0 (2mm) double-pointed needles. Rejoin yarn and pick up one extra stitch in the corner where the horn meets the small horn. Place a marker at the beginning of the round. 6 sts.
Rounds 1-5: Knit.
Cut a tail long enough to weave in. Pull it through all the stitches and remove them from the needles. Pull the tail tightly and secure. Weave in ends.

Nose
This pattern is crocheted in spiral. Don't join at the end of a row but continue working.
With the crochet hook and B: Ch3. Join with sl st to form ring.
Round 1: 5sc through ring.
Round 2: 2sc in each sc.
Round 3: 10sc.
End with sl st in next st to join. Fasten off, leaving a tail long enough for sewing.

FINISHING
1 Sew the nose onto the hat.
2 Fold the bottom of the ears and sew onto the hat.
3 Sew the antlers onto the hat.
4 Using D, embroider 2 small eyes in satin stitch.
5 Weave in ends.

The little mittens have all the features of the dearest reindeer hat.

MITTENS

(MAKE 2)

Cuff

Using US 0 (2mm) double-pointed needles and A, cast on 22 (24, 26) sts and divide evenly among 3 needles. Join to work in the round, being careful not to twist. Place a marker at the beginning of the round.

Rounds 1-10 (1-12, 1-14): Work in k1, p1 rib.

Thumb gusset

Switch to US 3 (3.25mm) double-pointed needles to work rest of mitten.

Round 1: M1R, knit to end of round. 23 (25, 27) sts.

Round 2: Knit.

Round 3: M1R, k1, M1L, knit to end of round. 25 (27, 29) sts.

Round 4: Knit.

Round 5: M1R, k3, M1L, knit to end of round. 27 (29, 31) sts.

Round 6: Knit.

Round 7: M1R, k5, M1L, knit to end of round. 29 (31, 33) sts.

Round 8: Knit.

Round (9, 9) (two larger sizes only): M1R, k7, M1L, knit to end of round. (33, 35) sts.

Round 9 (10, 10): K1, place 7 (9, 9) thumb stitches on waste yarn and rejoin to work hand stitches in the round, k21 (23, 25). 22 (24, 26) sts.

Rounds 10-22 (11-26, 11-28): Knit.

Closing up the top

Round 23 (27, 29): K2tog to end of round. 11 (12, 13) sts.

Round 24 (28, 30): Knit.

Round 25 (29, 31): K2tog to end of round. (If you get to the end of the round with only one stitch left, knit it.) 6 (6, 7) sts.

Cut a tail long enough to weave in. Pull it through all the stitches and remove them from the needles. Pull the tail tightly and secure. Weave in ends.

Thumb

Place 7 (9, 9) stitches from waste yarn onto US 3 (3.25mm) double-pointed needles. Rejoin yarn and pick up one extra stitch in the corner where the mitten meets the gusset. 8 (10, 10) sts.

Rounds 1-6 (1-6, 1-8): Knit.

Round 7 (7, 9): K2tog to end of round. 4 (5, 5) sts. Finish as for mitten Closing up the top.

Ears (make 2)

With the crochet hook and A: Ch6.

Row 1: 1hdc in 3rd ch from hook, 1hdc in each of next 2 ch, (3hdc, 1dc, 3hdc) all in last ch, (turn work so you are working on bottom of chain), 1hdc in each of next 3 ch.

Fasten off leaving a tail long enough for sewing.

Antlers (make 2)

With the crochet hook and C: Ch5.

Sl st in 2nd ch from hook,

Sl st in 3rd ch,

Sl st in 4th ch,

Sl st in 5th ch.

Fasten off, leaving a tail long enough for sewing.

FINISHING

1 Sew the ears onto the mittens.

2 Sew the antlers onto the mittens.

3 Using D, embroider 2 small eyes in satin stitch.

4 Using B, embroider the nose in satin stitch.

5 Weave in ends.

santa bear

Every child will adore this gorgeous Santa hat and mittens combo in cheery red and white. The pattern uses only straightforward knitting techniques.

COVERALL HAT AND MITTENS
LEVEL: beginner
SIZES
6-12 months (12-24 months, 2-3 years)
Finished measurements
From "cheek to cheek" around the hat:
14 (14½, 15)in. (36 [37, 38]cm)
Mitten circumference: 5½ (6, 6½)in.
(13.75 [15, 16.25]cm)
Mitten length: 5½ (6½, 7)in. (14 [16.5, 18]cm)
MATERIALS
HAT
Main yarn:
Color A: 1 x 3oz (85g) ball (135yd/123m)
Lion Brand Jiffy Yarn, 100% acrylic, True Red
Small amount:
Color B: Lion Brand Jiffy Yarn, 100% acrylic, White
Needles:
• 1 pair of US 3 (3.25mm) needles
• US 3 (3.25mm) circular needles
• 4 x US 3 (3.25mm) double-pointed needles
• Stitch marker
• Yarn needle
MITTENS
Main yarn:
Color A: 1 x 3oz (85g) ball (135yd/123m)
Lion Brand Jiffy Yarn, 100% acrylic, True Red
Small amount:
Color B: Lion Brand Jiffy Yarn, 100% acrylic, White
Needles:
• 4 x US 0 (2mm) double-pointed needles
• 4 x US 3 (3.25mm) double-pointed needles
• Yarn needle
GAUGE
16 sts and 25 rows = 4in./10cm square in stockinette stitch worked with US 3 (3.25mm) needles.
19 sts and 28 rows = 4in./10cm square in k1, p1 rib worked with US 3 (3.25mm) needles.

HAT

Using a pair of US 3 (3.25 mm) needles and A, cast on 57 (61, 65) sts.
Rows 1-6: K1, p1 rib.
Switch to B.
Rows 7- 30 (30, 32): Work in stockinette stitch, starting with a k row.
Row 31 (31, 33): K18 (19, 21), k2tog, k17 (19, 19), k2tog, turn. 55 (59, 63) sts.
Row 32 (32, 34): Sl, p17 (19, 19), p2tog, turn. 54 (58, 62) sts.
Row 33 (33, 35): Sl, k17 (19, 19), k2tog, turn. 53 (57, 61) sts.
Rep. rows 32 (32, 34) and 33 (33, 35) to row 54 (56, 62). 32 (34, 34) sts.
Row 55 (57, 63): Sl, *p1, k1* rep. from * to * 8 (9, 9) times, p1, k2tog, turn. 31 (33, 33) sts.
Row 56 (58, 64): Sl, *k1, p1* rep. from * to * 8 (9, 9) times, k1, p2tog, turn. 30 (32, 32) sts.
Rep. rows 55 (57, 63) and 56 (58, 64) to row 66 (68, 74). 20 (22, 22) sts.

Santa bear is irresistible and bound to prove popular throughout the festive season.

Neck ruff

Switch to US 3 (3.25 mm) circular needles. Place a marker at the beginning of the round.

Round 67 (69, 75): Sl, *p1, k1* rep. from * to * 8 (9, 9) times, p1, k2tog, pick up 13 (12, 12) sts on one side of the hat, cast on 7 sts, join to work in the round, being careful not to twist, pick up 13 (12, 12) sts on the other side of the hat. 52 (52, 52) sts.

Rounds 68-77 (70-81, 76-89): K1, p1 rib.

Round 78 (82, 90): K2 (3,3), *yo, k2, yo, k11* rep. from * to * 3 times, yo, k2, yo, k9 (8, 8). 60 (60, 60) sts.

Round 79 (83, 91): K3 (4, 4), *yo, k2, yo, k13* rep. from * to * 3 times, yo, k2, yo, k10 (9, 9). 68 (68, 68) sts.

Round 80 (84, 92): K4 (5, 5), yo, k2, yo, k15 (15, 15), yo, k2, yo, k15 (15, 15), yo, k2, yo, k15 (15, 15), yo, k2, yo, k11 (10, 10). 76 (76, 76) sts.

Round 81 (85, 93): K5 (6, 6), yo, k2, yo, k17 (17, 17), yo, k2, yo, k17 (17, 17), yo, k2, yo, k17 (17, 17), yo, k2, yo, k12 (11, 11). 84 (84, 84) sts.

Round 82 (86, 94): K6 (7, 7), yo, k2, yo, k19 (19, 19), yo, k2, yo, k19 (19, 19), yo, k2, yo, k19 (19, 19), yo, k2, yo, k13 (12, 12). 92 (92, 92) sts.

Round 83 (87, 95): K7 (8, 8), yo, k2, yo, k21 (21, 21), yo, k2, yo, k21 (21, 21), yo, k2, yo, k21 (21, 21), yo, k2, yo, k14 (13, 13). 100 (100, 100) sts.

Round (88, 96) (two larger sizes only): K (9, 9), yo, k2, yo, k (23, 23), yo, k2, yo, k (23, 23), yo, k2, yo, k (23, 23), yo, k2, yo, k (14, 14). (108, 108) sts.

Round (89, 97) (two larger sizes only): K (10, 10), yo, k2, yo, k (25, 25), yo, k2, yo, k (25, 25), yo, k2, yo, k (25, 25), yo, k2, yo, k (15, 15). (116, 116) sts.

Round (98) (largest size only): K (11), yo, k2, yo, k (27), yo, k2, yo, k (27), yo, k2, yo, k (27), yo, k2, yo, k (16). (124) sts.

Round (99) (largest size only): K (12), yo, k2, yo, k (29), yo, k2, yo, k (29), yo, k2, yo, k (29), yo, k2, yo, k (17). (132) sts.

Rounds 84-89 (90-95, 100-105) (all sizes): k1, p1 rib.

Bind off. Weave in ends.

Fold the ears as shown here and position them at the top of the head at the sides.

Fold the ear to the angle shown here and pin into position to sew.

Ears (make 2)

Using a pair of US 3 (3.25mm) needles and A, cast on 25 sts, leaving an 8in./20cm tail for sewing the ears in place.

Rows 1-5: K1, p1 rib.

Cut tail long enough to weave in. Pull through all 25 stitches, and remove them from the needle. Pull the tail tightly and secure. Make a strong knot.

FINISHING

1 Sew the ears to the hat in the position shown using an invisible seam.

2 Weave in ends.

MITTENS

(MAKE 2)

Cuff

Using US 0 (2 mm) double-pointed needles and B, cast on 22 (24, 26) sts and divide evenly among the 3 needles. Join to work in the round, being careful not to twist. Place a marker at the beginning of the round.

Rounds 1-10 (1-12, 1-14): K1, p1 rib.

Thumb gusset

Switch to US 3 (3.25mm) double-pointed needles and A to work rest of mitten.

Round 1: M1L, knit to end of round. 23 (25, 27) sts.

Round 2: Knit.

Round 3: M1L, K1, M1R, knit to end of round. 25 (27, 29) sts.

Round 4: Knit.

Round 5: M1L, K3, M1R, knit to end of round. 27 (29, 31) sts.

Round 6: Knit.

Round 7: M1L, k5, M1R, knit to end of round. 29 (31, 33) sts.

Round 8: Knit.

Round 9 (two larger sizes only): M1L, K7, M1R, knit to end of round. (33, 35) sts.

Round 9 (10, 10): K1, place 7 (9, 9) thumb stitches on waste yarn and rejoin to work hand stitches in the round, k21 (23, 25). 22 (24, 26) sts.

Rounds 10-22 (11-26, 11-28): Knit.

Closing up the top

Round 23 (27, 29): K2tog to end of round. 11 (12, 13) sts.

Round 24 (28, 30): Knit. 11 (12, 13) sts.

Round 25 (29, 31): K2tog to end of round. (If you get to the end of the round with only one stitch left, just knit it.) 6 (6, 7) sts.

Cut a tail long enough to weave in. Pull through all stitches. Remove them from the needles. Pull the tail tightly and secure. Weave in ends.

Thumb

Place 7 (9, 9) stitches from waste yarn onto US 3 (3.25mm) double-pointed needles. Rejoin yarn and pick up one extra stitch in the corner where the mitten meets the gusset. 8 (10, 10) sts.

Rounds 1-6 (1-6, 1-8): Knit.

Round 7 (7, 9): K2tog to end of round. 4 (5, 5) sts. Finish as for Mitten closing up the top.

The bold, bright mittens are in a classic style.

playful penguin

Playful penguin has a little Christmas hat to keep her warm, and two little chicks in the form of mittens. The hat is fastened under the chin with a crocheted button.

HAT, MITTENS, AND SCARF
LEVEL: intermediate
SIZES
6-12 months (12-24 months, 2-3 years)
Finished measurements
From "cheek to cheek" around the hat:
14 (14½, 15)in. (36 [37, 38]cm)
Mitten circumference: 5½ (6, 6½)in.
(13.75 [15, 16.25]cm)
Mitten length: 5½ (6½, 7)in. (14 [16.5, 18]cm)
Scarf length: 43in. (109cm)
Scarf width: 4in. (10cm)
MATERIALS
HAT
Main yarn:
Color A: 1 x 3oz (85g) ball (135yd/123m) Lion Brand Jiffy Yarn, 100% acrylic, Black
Small amounts:
Color B: Lion Brand Jiffy Yarn, 100% acrylic, White
Color C: Lion Brand Jiffy Yarn, 100% acrylic, True Red
Color D: Lion Brand Baby's First Yarn, 100% acrylic, Honey Bee
Needles:
• 1 pair of US 3 (3.25mm) needles
• 4 x US 3 (3.25mm) double-pointed needles
• Stitch marker
• US C-2 (2.75mm) crochet hook

• Yarn needle
• Small amount of toy stuffing
MITTENS
Main yarn:
Color A: 1 x 3oz (85g) ball (135yd/123m) Lion Brand Jiffy Yarn, 100% acrylic, Black
Small amounts:
Color B: Lion Brand Jiffy Yarn, 100% acrylic, White
Color D: Lion Brand Baby's First Yarn, 100% acrylic, Honey Bee
Needles:
• 4 x US 0 (2mm) double-pointed needles
• 4 x US 3 (3.25mm) double-pointed needles
• US C-2 (2.75mm) crochet hook
• Yarn needle
SCARF
Color C: 1 x 3oz (85g) ball (135yd/123m) Lion Brand Jiffy Yarn, 100% acrylic, True Red
Needles:
• 1 pair of US 3 (3.25mm) needles
• Yarn needle
GAUGE
16 sts and 25 rows = 4in./10cm square in stockinette stitch, worked with US 3 (3.25mm) needles.
19 sts and 28 rows = 4in./10cm square in k1, p1 rib, worked with US 3 (3.25mm) needles.

HAT

Using a pair of US 3 (3.25mm) needles and A, cast on 57 (61, 65) sts. Place a stitch marker at the beginning of the row.
Rows 1-6 (6, 6): K1, p1 rib.
Row 7: Knit.
Row 8: K6 (6, 6), p45 (49, 53), k6 (6, 6).
Rep. rows 7 and 8 to row 30 (30, 32).
Row 31 (31, 33): K18 (19, 21), k2tog, k17 (19, 19), k2tog, turn. 55 (59, 63) sts.
Row 32 (32, 34): Sl, p17 (19, 19), p2tog, turn. 54 (58, 62) sts.
Row 33 (33, 35): Sl, k17 (19, 19), k2tog, turn. 53 (57, 61) sts.
Rep. rows 32 (32, 34) and 33 (33, 35) to row 54 (58, 64). 32 (32, 32) sts.
Row 55 (59, 65): Sl, *p1, k1* rep. from * to * 8 (9, 9) times, p1, k2tog, turn. 31 (31, 31) sts.
Row 56 (60, 66): Sl, *k1, p1* rep. from * to * 8 (9, 9) times, k1, p2tog, turn. 30 (30, 30) sts.
Rep. rows 55 (59, 65) and 56 (60, 66) to row 66 (68, 74). 20 (22, 22) sts.
Cut yarn, leaving a long enough tail to weave in. Leave 20 (22, 22) sts on the needle.

Fastener

Rejoin the yarn at marker, push the crochet hook through at the marker from front to back and ch15.
1hdc in 5th ch from hook, 1hdc in next ch, ch2, skip 2 ch,
1hdc in each of next 6 ch, with right side facing insert hook into edge of rib row 3 and work 1sc, work a further 14 (14, 15) sc along bottom edge of hat (approximately in each alternate row) to sts held on needle, work 1sc into each of the 20 (22, 22) sts taking the sts off the needle one at a time, work a further 15 (15, 16) sc along bottom edge of hat (approximately in each alternate row) to front edge.
Fasten off. Weave in ends.

Christmas hat

With US 3 (3.25mm) double-pointed needles and B, cast on 22 sts and divide evenly among 3 needles. Join to work in the round, being careful not to twist. Place a marker at the beginning of the round.
Rounds 1-3: K1, p1 rib.
Switch to C.
Round 4: Knit.
Round 5: K2tog, k5, k2tog, k5, k2tog, k6. 19 sts.

The hat and scarf combination is just as cozy as a coverall hat.

Penguin chick faces with tiny
crocheted beaks and embroidered
eyes adorn the mittens.

Position the features as shown here,
with the Christmas hat slightly off
center.

Round 6: Knit.
Round 7: K2tog, k4, k2tog, k4, k2tog, k5. 16 sts.
Round 8: Knit.
Round 9: K2tog, k3, k2tog, k3, k2tog, k4. 13 sts.
Round 10: Knit.
Round 11: K2tog, k2, k2tog, k2, k2tog, k3. 10 sts.
Round 12: Knit.
Round 13: K2tog, k1, k2tog, k1, k2tog, k2. 7 sts.
Round 14: Knit.
Cut a tail long enough to weave in. Pull it through
all 7 stitches and remove them from the needles.
Pull the tail tightly and secure.

Pompom

With B, make a pompom 1in./2.5cm wide. See
page 140 for instructions, or use a pompom
maker.

Eyes (make 2)

This pattern is crocheted in spiral. Don't join at
the end of a row but continue working.
With the US C-2 (2.75mm) crochet hook and B:
Ch4. Join with sl st to form ring.
Round 1: 7sc through ring.
Round 2: 2sc in each sc. 14sc.
Round 3: 14sc.
Round 4: 14sc.
End with sl st in next st to join.
Fasten off, leaving a tail long enough for sewing.

Pupils (make 2)

With US US C-2 (2.75mm) crochet hook and A:
Ch4. Join with sl st to form ring.
Round 1: 7sc through ring.
End with sl st in next st to join.
Fasten off, leaving a tail long enough for sewing.

Beak

With US 3 (3.25mm) double-pointed needles
and D, cast on 16 sts. Join to work in the round,
being careful not to twist. Place a marker at the
beginning of the round.
Rounds 1-2: Knit.
Round 3: K2tog, k4, *k2tog* twice, k4, k2tog. 12 sts.
Round 4: Knit.
Round 5: K2tog, k2, *k2tog* twice, k2, k2tog. 8 sts.
Round 6: Knit.
Round 7: K2tog 4 times. 4 sts.
Cut a tail long enough to weave in. Pull it through
all 4 stitches and remove them from the needles.
Pull the tail tightly and secure.

Button

With US C-2 (2.75mm) crochet hook and C: Ch3.
Join with sl st to form ring.
Round 1: 5sc through ring.
End with sl st in next st to join, leaving an
8in./20cm tail for sewing the button in place.
Using a yarn needle or crochet hook pull the tail
through all 5 stitches. Pull the tail tightly and
secure. Make a strong knot.

FINISHING

1 Sew the pompom onto the Christmas hat.
2 Lightly stuff the Christmas hat.
3 Sew the Christmas hat onto the hat.
4 Sew the pupils onto the eyes.
5 Tuck the loose yarn ends into the dome of the
eyeball, and add a tiny bit of stuffing if you want.
6 With B embroider two small pupils (highlights)
in satin stitch.
7 Sew the eyes onto the hat.
8 Lightly stuff the beak.
9 Sew the beak onto the hat.
10 Sew the button onto the hat.
11 Weave in ends.

MITTENS

(MAKE 2)

Cuff

Using US 0 (2mm) double-pointed needles and A, cast on 22 (24, 26) sts and divide evenly among 3 needles. Join to work in the round, being careful not to twist. Place a marker at the beginning of the round.
Rounds 1-10 (1-12, 1-14): Work in k1, p1 rib.

Thumb gusset

Switch to US 3 (3.25mm) double-pointed needles to work rest of mitten.
Round 1: M1R, knit to end of round. 23 (25, 27) sts.
Round 2: Knit.
Round 3: M1R, k1, M1L, knit to end of round. 25 (27, 29) sts.
Round 4: Knit.
Round 5: M1R, k3, M1L, knit to end of round. 27 (29, 31) sts.
Round 6: Knit.
Round 7: M1R, k5, M1L, knit to end of round. 29 (31, 33) sts.
Round 8: Knit.
Round (9, 9) (two larger sizes only): M1R, k7, M1L, knit to end of round. (33, 35) sts.
Round 9 (10, 10): K1, place 7 (9, 9) thumb stitches on waste yarn and rejoin to work hand stitches in the round, k21 (23, 25). 22 (24, 26) sts.
Rounds 10-19 (11-23, 11-25): Knit.
Switch to B.

Rounds 19-22 (23-26, 25-28): Knit.
Closing up the top
Round 23 (27, 29): K2tog to end of round. 11 (12, 13) sts.
Round 24 (28, 30): Knit.
Round 25 (29, 31): K2tog to end of round. (If you get to the end of the round with only one stitch left, knit it.) 6 (6, 7) sts.
Cut a tail long enough to weave in. Pull it through all the stitches and remove them from the needles. Pull the tail tightly and secure. Weave in ends.

Thumb

Place 7 (9, 9) stitches from waste yarn onto US 3 (3.25mm) double-pointed needles. Rejoin yarn and pick up one extra stitch in the corner where the mitten meets the gusset. 8 (10, 10) sts.
Rounds 1-6 (1-6, 1-8): Knit.
Round 7 (7, 9): K2tog to end of round. 4 (5, 5) sts.
Finish as for mitten Closing up the top.

Beak

With the crochet hook and D, 4ch, 1sl st in 2nd ch from the hook, 1sc in 3rd ch from the hook, 1hdc in 4th ch from the hook. Fasten off, leaving a tail long enough for sewing

FINISHING

1 With A embroider the foreheads in satin stitch.
2 Embroider eyes using A.
3 Sew the beaks onto the mittens.
4 Weave in ends.

SCARF

Using a pair of US 3 (3.25mm) needles and C, cast on 17 sts and divide evenly among 3 needles. Join to work in the round, being careful not to twist. Place a marker at the beginning of the round.
Rows 1-8: Garter st.
Row 9: K1, k2tog, k11, k2tog, k1. 15 sts.
Rows 10-13: Garter st.
Row 14: K1, k2tog, k9, k2tog, k1. 13 sts.
Rows 15-18: Garter st.
Row 19: K1, k2tog, k7, k2tog, k1. 11 sts.
Rows 20-23: Garter st.
Row 24: K1, k2tog, k5, k2tog, k1. 9 sts.
Rows 25-28: Garter st.
Row 29: K1, M1, k7, M1, k1. 11 sts.
Rows 30-33: Garter st.
Row 34: K1, M1, k9, M1, k1. 13 sts.
Rows 35-38: Garter st.
Row 39: K1, M1, k11, M1, k1. 15 sts.
Rows 40-43: Garter st.
Row 44: K1, M1, k13, M1, k1. 17 sts.
Row 45-63: Garter st.
Rows 64-99: Rep. rows 9-44. 17 sts.
Rows 100-169: Garter st.
Rows 170-279: Rep. rows *9-63* twice.
Bind off. Weave in ends.

The scarf is knitted in garter stitch in an unusual wavy shape.

knitting basics

before you start

TOOLS

Before you start knitting, gather together everything you will need for your project. For every *Monster Knits* project, you will need the following:

- **Knitting needles:** check the type you need for each pattern (straight, double-pointed, or circular) and the sizes required
- **Small pair of sharp scissors**, used only for yarns
- **Needle gauge ruler or tape measure** for measuring the stitches and rows in the gauge swatch before you start knitting your project
- **Stitch marker:** when knitting in the round, you will need to mark the beginning of the round
- **Pen or pencil** for keeping track of where you are in the pattern
- **Yarn needle** for sewing up your project at the end

For some projects you will need:
- **Crochet hook:** check size required
- **Cable needle:** this is a short needle used to hold stitches temporarily while you are forming the cable

SIZING

The patterns in this book are written for three sizes: 6-12 months, 12-24 months, and 2-3 years. Coverall hats cover the entire head and part of the face, so the measurement given in the patterns is from cheek to cheek around the hat. To make sure you are knitting the right size, measure the circumference of your child's head from cheek to cheek at the widest point, just above the ears. To check mitten size, measure the circumference of the hand at the widest point, and the length of the hand. If your child is between sizes, it is best to knit the larger size.

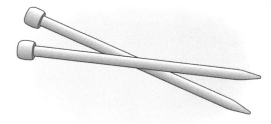

BAMBOO NEEDLES

METAL NEEDLES

TAPESTRY NEEDLE

YARNS

SELECTION

All the yarns in this book have been chosen because they are soft and comfortable to wear as well as being extremely warm. For the best results, it is best to purchase exactly the yarn stated in the pattern. Make sure that you buy enough wool for your project, and always check the shade and dye lot number on the ball band to ensure that each ball is the same color.

SUBSTITUTION

If you do need to substitute a yarn, always buy another yarn of the same weight as the one in the pattern. Knit swatches until you achieve the correct pattern gauge. You will need to figure out how much of the substitute yarn you will need. The patterns provide the amounts of yarn in both weight and length to help you to do this.

Note that if you select a different fiber, this can affect the design. It is best to stick to the acrylic fibers suggested in the patterns.

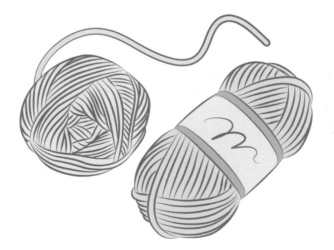

READING PATTERNS

If you are knitting patterns for the first time, take time to familiarize yourself with the abbreviations on page 142 and check that you can do all the stitches in the pattern. See pages 120 to 131 for explanations of the basic knitting techniques and pages 132 to 135 for crochet techniques. A few basic embroidery stitches are required for some patterns (see page 137). You may like to practice some of the stitches on a swatch before starting your project.

Note that the instructions are given for the smallest size first, with the two larger sizes in parentheses. Where two figures in parentheses are given, the row or round applies to the two larger sizes only. Where just one figure in parentheses appears, the row or round applies to the largest size alone. Before you start, it is advisable to photocopy the pattern and highlight the instructions for the size you are making.

Always check the actual size of the finished pattern before you start, and check the size will fit your child. You may like to adjust the pattern slightly; for example, if your child has long hands, you could knit a few more rows on the mittens.

make sure you have all measurements, equipment and materials before you start

smallest size first, with the two larger sizes in parentheses

use the photos as a guide when making up the garment

sleepy bluebird

An easy-to-knit beak and some basic embroidery transform this simple project into a stylish set. The hat decoration is repeated smaller on the mittens.

COVERALL HAT AND MITTENS
LEVEL: beginner
SIZES
6–12 months (1–2 years, 2–3 years)
Finished measurements
From 'cheek to cheek' around the hat:
36, 37, 38cm (14, 14½, 15in)
Mitten circumference: 13.5–15, 16.25cm (5½–6, 6½in)
Mitten length: 14, 16.5, 19cm
(5½, 6½in, 7½in)
MATERIALS
HAT
Main yarn:
Colour A: 1 x 40g (3oz) ball (120m) Wyd's
Lion Brand Jiffy Yarn, 100% acrylic,
Pastel Blue
Small amounts:
Colour B: Lion Brand Jiffy Yarn, 100%
acrylic, Blossom
Colour C: Lion Brand Jiffy Yarn, 100%
acrylic, Black
Needles:
• 1 pair of UK 10 (3.25mm) needles
• 1 UK 10 (3.25mm) circular needle
• 4 x UK 10 (3.25mm) double-pointed needles
• Stitch marker
• Yarn needle
• Small amount of toy stuffing
MITTENS
Main yarn:
Colour A: 1 x 85g (3oz) ball (145m) (90yd)
Lion Brand Jiffy Yarn, 100% acrylic,
Pastel Blue
Small amounts:
Colour B: Lion Brand Jiffy Yarn, 100%
acrylic, Blossom
Colour C: Lion Brand Jiffy Yarn, 100%
acrylic, Black
Needles:
• 4 x UK 12mm double-pointed needles
• 4 x UK 10 (3.25mm) double-pointed
needles
• Yarn needle
TENSION
15 sts and 25 rows = 10cm (4in square)
in stocking stitch worked with UK 10
(3.25mm) needles
19 sts and 28 rows = 10cm (4in square) in
stocking stitch worked with UK 10 (3.25mm) needles

HAT
Using colour A and UK 10 (3.25mm) needles cast on 57 (61, 65) sts.
Rows 1–6 (6, 6): k1 p1 rib.
Rows 7–30 (30, 32): Work in stocking stitch starting with a k row.
Row 31 (31, 33): K45 (49, 21), k2tog, k17 (19, 19), k2tog, turn. 55 (59, 63) sts.
Row 32 (32, 34): Sl, p11 (19, 19), p2tog, turn. 54 (58, 62) sts.
Row 33 (33, 35): Sl, k11 (19, 19), k2tog, turn. 53 (57, 61) sts.
Rep rows 31 (32, 34) and 33 (33, 35) to make up to 28 (30, 32) sts.
Row 55 (57, 63): Sl, *k4, k4* rep from * to * (6 (6, 9) times), k1, k2tog, turn. p1 (33, 33) sts.
Row 56 (58, 64): Sl, *k1, p1* rep, from * to * (9 (9) times), k1 p2tog, turn. 30 (32, 32) sts.
Rep rows 45 (57, 63) and 56 (58, 64) to make up to 68, (45, 20) (22, 22) sts.

Neck ruff
Switch to a UK 10 (3.25mm) circular needle.
Place a marker at the beginning of the round.
Pick up and knit 67 (69, 75) sts at right edge from 1 to 4 (13, 4) times of k2tog, pick up 1 (12, 12) sts on each side of the hat. Cast on 7 (5, 7, 7), sts and work in the round, being careful not to twist, pick up 1 (12, 12) sts on the other side of the hat. 62 (52, 52) sts.
Rounds 68–77 (70–81, 76–89): k1, p1 rib.
Round 78 (82, 90): K2, (5, 2), *k2, k2 st* k2 (4, 6) to p2, yo, k3, yo, k3 (3, 5), yo, k2 k2, k3 (3, 3) yo, k2, yo, k9 (11, 11), yo k2 xo.
Round 79 (83, 91): k3 (4, 4), yo, k2, yo, k3 (3, 5), yo, k2, yo, k3 (3, 5), yo, k2, yo, k6 (6, 6) yo.

The beak is lightly stuffed so that it stands up on the hat.

GAUGE

To achieve the correct size, it is important to knit to the gauge specified in the pattern. If the gauge is too loose, the garment will have an uneven shape, causing problems with the fit. If it is too tight, the fabric can become hard and inflexible. The gauge details for each pattern specify the gauge in both stockinette and rib stitch. Always make a sample to check the gauge before you start, using the correct yarn, needle size, and stitch pattern.

Knit a sample of at least 5in./13cm. Smooth it out on a flat surface, without stretching it. Mark 4in./10cm with pins and count the number of stitches between the pins. This is the stitch gauge. Then mark 4in./10cm vertically with pins, and count the number of rows. This is your row gauge. If you have more stitches and rows than indicated, the gauge is too tight. Knit a new sample using larger needles. If you have fewer stitches and rows, the gauge is too loose, and you should knit a new sample with smaller needles.

STITCH GAUGE

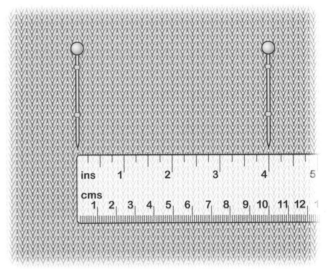

ROW GAUGE

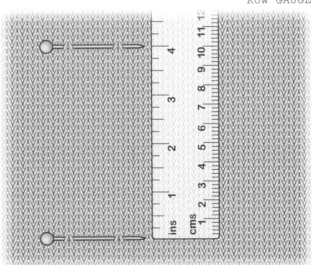

casting on

When you start knitting, the first step is to make a slip knot. Then you create a foundation row, known as a cast-on row. There are several ways of creating this row. Two of the most popular methods are described here: thumb cast on and cable cast on.

slip knot

1 Make a circle of yarn around the fingers of your left hand. Use the knitting needle to pull a loop of the yarn attached to the ball through the yarn circle.

2 Pull both ends of the yarn to make a tight knot on the knitting needle. This is a slip knot.

STEP 1

STEP 2

thumb cast on

This one-needle method gives a flexible edge with some give. Since you will be working toward the yarn end, ensure you have sufficient yarn for the cast-on row. Leave more yarn than you need; any excess can be used later for sewing up.

1 Make a slip knot (see opposite page), allowing a long tail. Hold the slip knot on the needle in your right hand and the yarn from the ball over your index finger. Wind the tail end of the yarn over your left thumb from front to back, securing the yarn in your palm.

2 Insert the knitting needle upward through the yarn loop on your left thumb.

3 Use the right index finger to wind the yarn from the ball over the knitting-needle point.

4 Bring the yarn through the loop on your thumb to make a stitch on the knitting needle. Allow the loop of yarn to slip off the left thumb. Pull the loose end to tighten the stitch. Repeat these steps until you have the correct number of stitches.

STEP 1

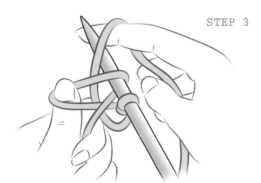

STEP 2

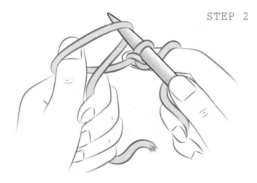

STEP 3

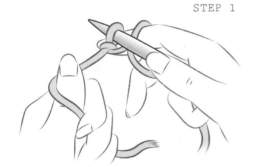

STEP 4

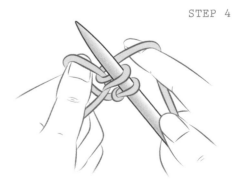

cable cast on

This two-needle method provides a strong yet flexible edge, and is excellent for ribbed edges. It is one of the most popular cast-on methods. **Do not make the new stitches too tight**; you will need to insert the needle between them to make the next stitch.

1 Make a slip knot (see page 120). With the needle with the slip knot in the left hand, insert the other needle from right to left, and front to back, through the slip knot. Bring the yarn from the ball up and over the right-hand needle.

2 Using the right-hand needle, draw a loop through the slip stitch to create another stitch. Slip the new stitch onto the left-hand needle.

3 Insert the right-hand needle between the two stitches on the left-hand needle. Bring the yarn around the point of the right-hand needle.

4 Pull the yarn through to create a new stitch. Place the new stitch on the left-hand needle. Repeat steps 3 and 4 until you have cast on the correct number of stitches.

STEP 1

STEP 2

STEP 3

STEP 4

knitting techniques

knit stitch (k)

Knit stitch is the first stitch to learn. If you work knit stitch continuously, it forms garter stitch (see page 129).

1 Hold the needle with the cast-on stitches in your left hand. Insert the right-hand needle from right to left, front to back, through the first stitch.

2 Hold the yarn from the ball on your left-hand index finger. Bring this yarn around the point of the right-hand needle.

3 Bring the right-hand needle and yarn through the stitch to form a new stitch on the right-hand needle. Slip the original stitch off the left-hand needle.

Repeat these steps until you have worked all of the stitches on the left-hand needle. You have completed one knit row.

STEP 1

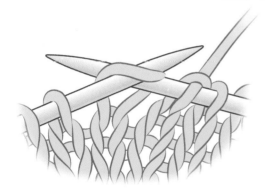

STEP 2

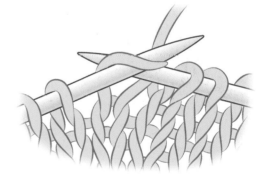

STEP 3

purl stitch (p)

Purl is the next stitch to learn. When knit and purl stitch are worked in alternate rows, they form stockinette stitch (see page 129), which is used for all the patterns in this book.

1 Hold the yarn in front of the right-hand needle. Insert the right-hand needle from right to left into the front of the first stitch on the left-hand needle.

2 Hold the yarn from the ball on your left-hand index finger. Bring this yarn around the point of the right-hand needle.

3 Bring the right-hand needle and yarn through the stitch to form a new stitch on the right-hand needle. Slip the original stitch off the left-hand needle.

Repeat these steps until you have worked all of the stitches on the left-hand needle. You have completed one purl row.

STEP 1

STEP 2

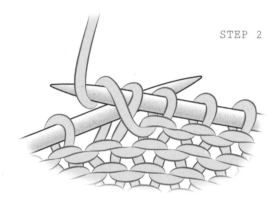

STEP 3

increase

You increase stitches to add width to the knitted fabric, for example, when creating the thumb gusset on the mittens. There are two ways to increase stitches in *Monster Knits*; the patterns indicate which method to use.

MAKE ONE (M1)

1 Insert the left-hand needle from front to back below the horizontal strand of wool in between the stitch you have just worked on the right-hand needle and the first stitch on the left-hand needle.

2 Knit into the back of the loop. Drop the strand from the left-hand needle. You have created an additional stitch on the right-hand needle.

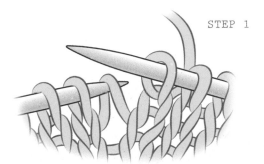

STEP 1

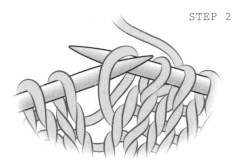

STEP 2

YARN OVER (YO)

1 Yarn over between knit stitches
Take the yarn forward between the needles, from the back to the front of your knitting. Take the yarn over the right-hand needle and knit the next stitch.

2 Yarn over between purl stitches
Bring the yarn from the right-hand needle to the back, and between the needles to the front. Purl the next stitch.

3 Yarn over between a purl and a knit stitch
Bring the yarn from the front over the right-needle to the back. Knit the next stitch.

4 Yarn over between a knit and a purl stitch
Take the yarn forward between the needles from the back to the front of your knitting. Take the yarn over the top of the right-hand needle to the back. Then bring it forward between the needles. Purl the next stitch.

STEP 1

STEP 2

STEP 3

STEP 4

decrease

You decrease stitches to make the fabric narrower, for example, when shaping the bottom of a hat. There are two ways to decrease stitches in *Monster Knits*; the patterns indicate which method to use.

1 KNIT TWO TOGETHER (K2TOG)
This is done on a knit row. Place the right-hand needle from right to left though the next two stitches on the left-hand needle. Knit them together. You have decreased by one stitch.

2 PURL TWO TOGETHER (P2TOG)
This is done on a purl row. Insert the right-hand needle from right to left through the next two stitches on the left-hand needle. Purl them together. You have decreased by one stitch.

STEP 1

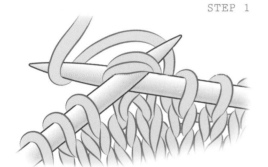

STEP 2

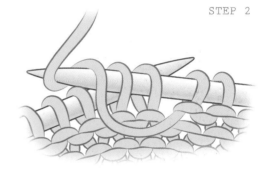

bind off

Binding off is the last row of your knitting. Ensure that the bind off is firm but flexible so that hats, mittens, and booties can be easily pulled on and off. Always bind off in the pattern you are using.

KNIT BIND OFF

1 Knit two stitches as normal. Insert the left-hand needle into the first stitch you knitted on the right-hand needle and lift it over the second stitch, and off the needle.

2 You now have one stitch on the right-hand needle. Knit the next stitch. Repeat step 1 until you have bound off all of the stitches and have one stitch left on the needle. Pull the yarn through the last stitch to fasten off.

PURL BIND OFF

1 Purl two stitches as normal. Insert the left-hand needle into the back of the first stitch you knitted on the right-hand needle and lift it over the second stitch, and off the needle.

2 You now have one stitch on the right-hand needle. Purl the next stitch. Repeat step 1 until you have bound off all of the stitches and have one stitch left on the needle. Pull the yarn through the last stitch to fasten off.

KNIT BIND OFF

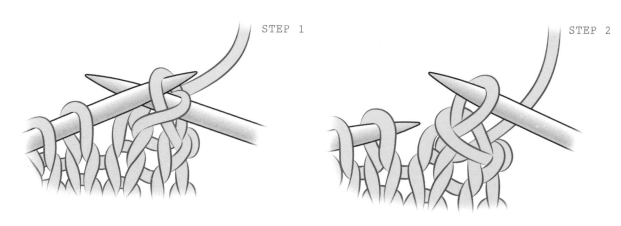

STEP 1

STEP 2

PURL BIND OFF

STEP 1

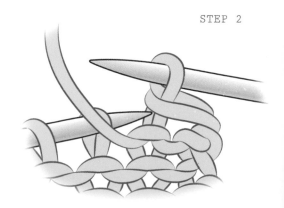

STEP 2

knitting stitches

STOCKINETTE STITCH

This is the most common pattern in *Monster Knits*. To create stockinette stitch, knit alternate knit and purl rows. In this book, the knit side is the right side of the fabric.

Cast on the number of stitches required.

Row 1: Knit.

Row 2: Purl.

Repeats rows 1 and 2 to form stockinette stitch.

SINGLE RIB STITCH

Monster Knits patterns use k1 p1 rib (single rib). You make the rib by alternating knit and purl stitches in the row, to create vertical columns of knit and purl stitches. The rib has an elastic quality that makes it suitable for areas that need to stretch, such as mitten cuffs.

Cast on an even number of stitches.

Row 1: *K1, p1, repeat from * to end.

Repeat this row to form a single rib pattern.

DOUBLE RIB STITCH

A k2, p2 double rib is used to make the baby bear hat and mittens.

Cast on a multiple of 4 stitches and 2 more:

Row 1: K2, *p2, k2, repeat from * to end.

Row 2: P2, *k2, p2, repeat from * to end.

Repeat rows 1 and 2 to form double rib.

GARTER STITCH

To make garter stitch, use knit stitch for all the rows.

Cast on the number of stitches required.

Row 1: Knit.

Repeat row 1 to form garter stitch.

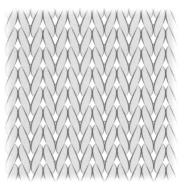

STOCKINETTE STITCH

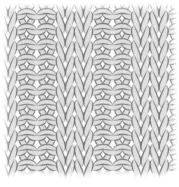

DOUBLE RIB STITCH

SINGLE RIB STITCH

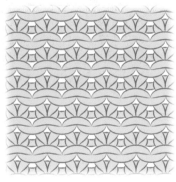

GARTER STITCH

cables

To form a cable, you cross one set of stitches over another. The cable forms a vertical rope of stockinette stitch and makes an attractive pattern, for example, on the Alien Elf hat (see page 56).

BACK CROSS CABLE
1 Move the first two cable stitches purlwise from the left-hand needle onto the cable needle.

2 With the cable needle at the back of the knitting, knit the next two stitches on the left-hand needle. Make sure that you keep the yarn tight to prevent gaps. Knit the two stitches from the cable needle. You have made the cable cross.

STEP 1

STEP 2

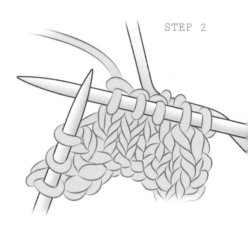

FRONT CROSS CABLE
1 Move the first two cable stitches purlwise from the left-hand needle onto the cable needle. With the cable needle at the front of the work, knit the next two stitches on the left-hand needle. Make sure that you keep the yarn tight to prevent gaps.

2 Knit the two stitches from the cable needle. You have made the cable cross.

STEP 1

STEP 2

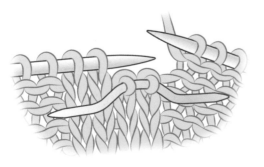

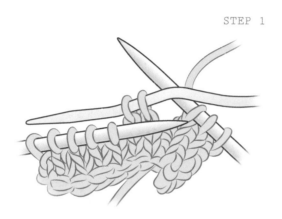

picking up stitches

When you are making the neck ruffs of a *Monster Knits* hat, you will need to pick up stitches from the sides of the hat. The pattern will indicate how many stitches you need to pick up.

ALONG A SELVEDGE

Work with the right side of the knitting facing you. Insert the needle from front to back in between the first and the second stitches of the first row. Bring the yarn around the needle and pull a loop through to create a new stitch on the needle. Repeat along the edge of the knitting.

knitting in the round

For the patterns in this book, four needles are used to knit in the round. Divide the stitches evenly over three needles to form a triangle. Before knitting, make sure that the cast-on edge is not twisted. Use a stitch marker to mark the beginning of the round.

Start knitting the stitches with the fourth needle. As each needle becomes free, use it to knit the stitches from the next needle. When you transfer from one needle to the next, pull the yarn firmly; this prevents a run from forming.

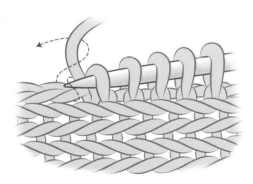

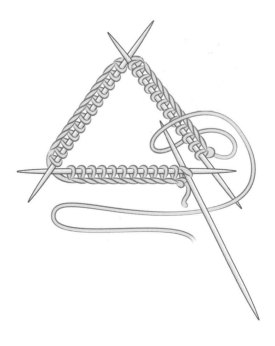

crochet stitches

To make some of the *Monster Knits* projects, you will need to be able to crochet. All the stitches you'll need are explained here.

Most people like to hold the crochet hook like a knife or pencil, but you can experiment to find out the most comfortable way.

SLIP KNOT

Every piece of crochet starts with a slip knot.

1 Make a loop in the yarn.

2 Use the hook to catch the ball end of the yarn. Draw it through the loop.

3 Pull on the yarn and hook to tighten the knot.

SLIP KNOT

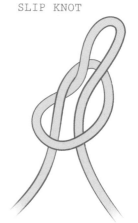

STEP 2

MAKING A CHAIN (CH)

This is the first row of a piece of crochet.

1 Make a slip knot, as above.

2 Hold the end of the yarn attached to the crochet hook with the left hand.

3 Pass the hook in front of the yarn, under, and around it.

4 Pull the hook and yarn through the loop formed by the slip knot.

5 Repeat steps 2 to 4 until you have the correct number of chain stitches.

MAKING A CHAIN

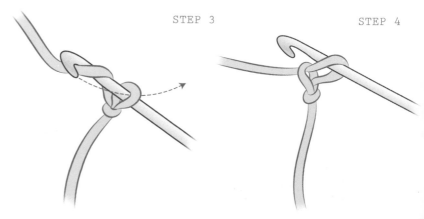

STEP 3   STEP 4

SLIP STITCH (SL ST)

You need a slip stitch to join one stitch to another, usually to join a circle.

1 Insert the hook into the loops of the next stitch. (If you are joining the starting chain, as here, just insert the hook into the back loop.)

2 Pass the yarn over the hook (yoh), as for the chain stitch and draw it through both stitches.

Slip stitch in a row

To make a slip stitch in a row, insert the hook through the two loops of the next stitch as below and follow step **2**.

STEP 1

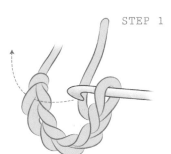

STEP 2

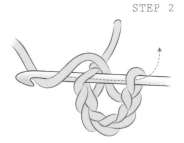

SINGLE CROCHET (SC)

This is a dense stitch commonly used in decorations for hats and mittens.

1 Insert the hook into the next stitch, front to back. Place the yarn over the hook (yoh).

2 Draw the hook through one loop to the front, leaving two loops on the hook. Yoh.

3 Draw the hook through the two remaining loops to finish the stitch.

STEP 1

STEP 3

DOUBLE CROCHET (DC)

Double crochet creates a more open stitch than single crochet.

1 Wrap the yarn over the hook (yoh) from the front to the back.

2 Insert the hook into the next stitch, from the front to the back.

3 Yoh. Draw through the stitch, leaving three loops on the hook.

4 Yoh again. Pull through the first two loops.

5 Yoh and draw through the last two loops.

HALF-DOUBLE CROCHET (HDC)

This stitch is half the height of a double crochet. In step 4, draw the hook through all the loops in one go.

STEP 1

STEP 4

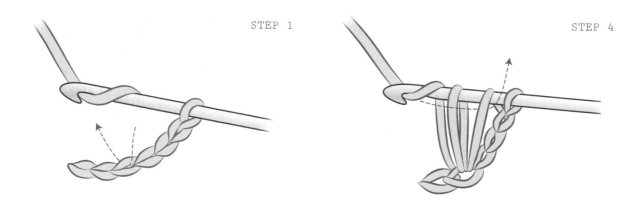

STEP 5

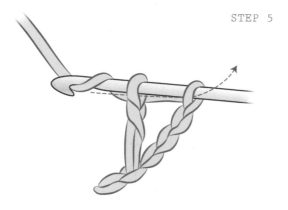

finishing crochet and weaving in

FINISHING OFF

I Finish the last stitch.

2 Cut the yarn, leaving a tail of 2–3in./5–8cm.

3 Wrap the yarn over the hook, and pull the tail through the final loop on the hook.

4 Pull the tail tight to fasten the knot.

WEAVING IN

1 Thread the tail of the yarn into a yarn needle.

2 Thread the needle down the side of the work at the edge.

3 Pull the tail all the way through.

STEP 2

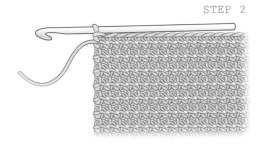

STEP 1

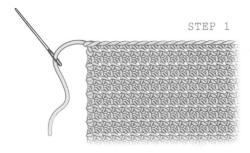

STEP 3

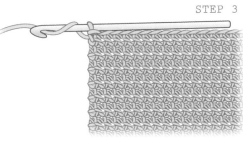

STEP 2

STEP 4

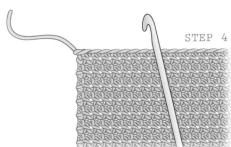

STEP 3

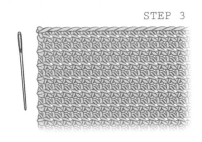

sewing stitches

Sewing up your project is an important stage of the job, which affects the look of the garment. When you cast on, it is wise to leave a long tail to use later for sewing up your project. If you have not done this, when you secure the thread for the seam, allow a length of yarn that you can darn in afterward.

The pattern instructions indicate when you should sew up the elements of the garment. In *Monster Knits*, the grafting method is used to join up two bound-off edges. Always sew your seams with a blunt yarn or tapestry needle, which will not split and damage the yarn.

grafting

1 Butt the two bound-off edges together. Bring the needle out in the center of the first stitch, just below the bound-off edge on one piece. Put the needle through the middle of the first stitch on the second piece, and take it out through the middle of the next stitch.

2 Put the needle through the center of the first stitch of the first piece once again. Take it out through the center of the stitch next to it. Continue to sew in this way to end of the seam.

STEP 1

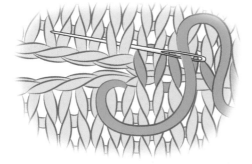

STEP 2

embroidery

The projects in this book use some basic embroidery stitches, for example, to embroider the smiling mouth of funky frog (see page 92). The yarn you need will be specified for each project. You'll also need a yarn needle.

STRAIGHT STITCH

Pass the needle in and out of the fabric. Make sure the surface stitches are the same length. The stitches underneath should be of equal length, but about half the size of the surface stitches.

BACKSTITCH

This method shows how to do backstitch from right to left.

1 Bring up the needle at 1 and make a stitch going to the right (2).

2 Now bring up the needle to the left of the beginning of the first stitch, at stitch-length distance (3).

3 Make a stitch going to the right, which meets the start of the first stitch (1).

4 Repeat the process to the end of the row.

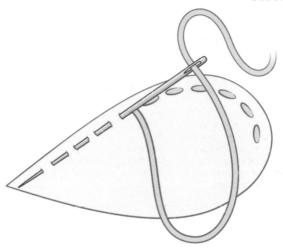

STRAIGHT STITCH

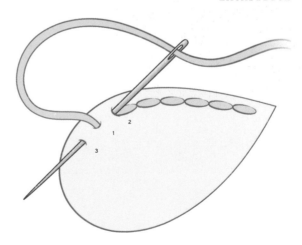

BACKSTITCH

finishing and care

close fins and ears

The following patterns use this technique to close the fins and ears: cute shark hat, little red rooster hat, furry fox hat and mittens, dinky dragon hat and mittens, wise owl hat and mittens. Before you start one of these projects, practice this technique by following the instructions here:

Cast on 21 sts.
Rows 1-4: Stockinette stitch.
Row 5: K10, yo, k1, yo, k10. (23 sts)
Row 6: P11, yo, p1, yo, p11. (25 sts)
Row 7: K12, yo, k1, yo, k12. (27 sts) (Step A)
Row 8: P13, yo, p1, yo, p13. (29 sts)
Row 9: K14, yo, k1, yo, k14. (31 sts)
Row 10: P15, yo, p1, yo, p15. (33 sts)
Row 11: K16, yo, k1, yo, k16. (35 sts)
Row 12: P17, yo, p1, yo, p17. (37 sts)
Row 13: K18, yo, k1, yo, k18. (39 sts)
Row 14: P19, yo, p1, yo, p19. (41 sts)
Row 15: K10, sl next 10 sts, fold right-hand and left-hand needles parallel to each other with wrong sides facing and points facing to the right (right-hand needle is at the back), slip next st on left-hand needle onto a crochet hook; it will be 21st st in row.

Insert crochet hook into 20th st (next st on the right-hand needle—step B), slip it off the needle onto the hook and pull this st through the loop on the hook. (Step C)

Continue in this way:
****insert hook into next st on left-hand needle (step D), slip it off the needle onto the hook and pull this st through the st already on hook, insert hook into next st on right-hand needle, slip it off the needle onto the hook and pull this st through the st already on hook, **
repeat from ** to ** until the last slipped st on the right-hand needle (11th st) has been pulled through the next st on the left-hand needle, insert hook into next st on left-hand needle, slip it off the needle onto the hook and pull this st through st already on hook, slip st from crochet hook back onto the left-hand needle, unfold needles and hold normally, k11. 21sts

A Row 7: K12, yo, K1, yo, K12. (27 sts)
B Insert the hook into the next stitch on the right-hand needle (20th st in row)
C Pull 20th st through 21st st
D Insert the hook into the next st on the left-hand needle.

A

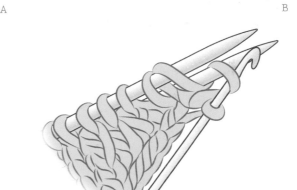

B

C

D

pompoms

Pompoms make delightful decorative details and are used on the sweet snowman and playful penguin. Since these garments are for very young children, make sure to bind the pompom tightly so that little fingers cannot pull it apart.

1 Cut out two circles of card the same size. They should be slightly smaller than the size of the pompom required. Cut a hole in the middle of each circle. Hold the circles together. Thread a darning needle with yarn. Wind it around the center and outer edges until you have closed the hole.

2 Insert a pair of small, sharp scissors in between the two card circles and cut the wool between them.

3 Firmly tie a piece of yarn in the middle of the two card circles. Remove the card circles.

STEP 1

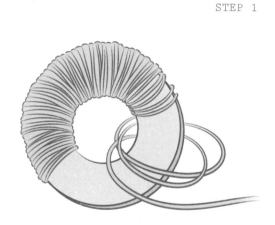

STEP 2

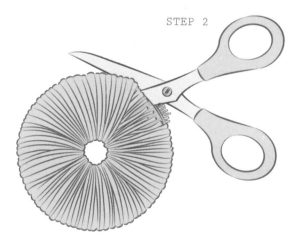

STEP 3

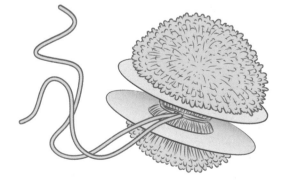

GARMENT CARE

You will want to take care of your beautiful hand knits so that they last as long as possible. Bear in mind that garments for young children will have to be washed frequently, so it is important to follow the washing instructions carefully.
All the yarns in this book are machine washable. Always check the ball band for washing instructions.

If you decide to hand wash your knits, ensure you use a mild detergent designed for knitwear, and warm rather than hot water. Immerse the garment in the water and squeeze it very gently to release the dirt. Avoid rubbing or agitating it. Once washed and rinsed, carefully squeeze out the water before taking it out of the bowl. Roll it in a towel to remove excess water.

Whether machine or hand washed, it is best to dry hand knits flat on a towel or other absorbent cloth. You can pat the garment back into shape while it is still damp. Never dry your hand knits on a radiator or other direct heat source.

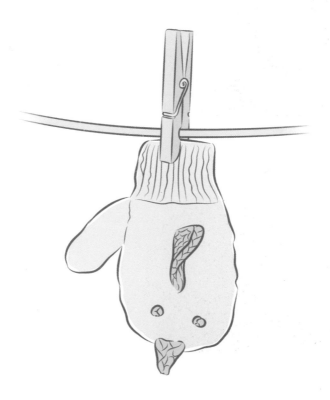

abbreviations + conversions

KNITTING ABBREVIATIONS

cn cable needle
k knit
k2tog knit next two stitches together as one
M1 make one by inserting left-hand needle from front to back under the horizontal strand between the stitch just worked on the right-hand needle and the first stitch on the left-hand needle, and knitting into the back of the loop to form a new stitch on the right-hand needle.
M1L pick up the second stitch below the first stitch on the left needle, place it onto the left needle and then knit into it; knit the first stitch on the left needle.
M1R knit the first stitch on the left needle (now this stitch will be placed on the right needle), pick up the second stitch below the first stitch on the right needle, place it on the left needle and knit into it.
p purl
p2tog purl next two stitches together as one
rep repeat
sl slip next stitch onto the right-hand needle without knitting or purling
st(s) stitch(es)
yo yarn over
* * repeat directions between *** *** as many times as indicated

CROCHET ABBREVIATIONS

ch chain stitch
sc single crochet
sl st slip stitch
skip2 skip two stitches
dc double crochet
3dc three double crochets in same stitch
hdc half double crochet

KNITTING NEEDLES

Metric	US	UK
2mm	0	14
2.25mm	1	13
2.75mm	2	12
3mm	-	11
3.25mm	3	10
3.5mm	4	-
3.75mm	5	9
4mm	6	8
4.5mm	7	7
5mm	8	6
5.5mm	9	5
6mm	10	4
6.5mm	10.5	3
7mm	10.5	2
7.5mm	11	1
8mm	13	0
10mm	15	000

CROCHET HOOKS

US	Metric	UK
C-2	2.75mm	-
-	3mm	11

resources

YARNS

A.C. Moore
www.acmoore.com
Tel: 1-888-ACMOORE
Needle arts, knit and crochet, yarn, and tools

Etsy
www.etsy.com
Online market for handmade and vintage goods, and supplies

Joann Fabric and Craft Stores
www.joann.com
Jo-Ann Fabric and Craft Stores(R)
5555 Darrow Road
Hudson, Ohio 44236
Tel: 1-888-739-4120
Fabric, sewing, and needle arts supplies

Knitting-Warehouse
www.knitting-warehouse.com
Corporate Office Address:
Beverly Fabrics Inc., Knitting-Warehouse.com
9019 Soquel Dr.
Aptos, CA 95003
Tel: 1-831-728-2584
Discount knitting and crochet supplies, yarn, and notions

Lion Brand Yarn
www.lionbrand.com
135 Kero Road
Carlstadt, NJ 07072
Tel: 1-800-258-9276
Yarn, tools, books, patterns

Michael's
www.michaels.com
1-800-MICHAELS
Knit and crochet, yarn, and tools

Yarn Market
www.yarnmarket.com
12936 Stonecreek Drive, Unit D
Pickerington, OH
Tel: 1-614-861-7223
Yarn, tools, and books

KNITTING COMMUNITY

Ravelry
www.ravelry.com
Community for knitters and crocheters; free to join

BOOKS
200 Knitting Tips, Techniques & Trade Secrets: An Indispensable Reference of Technical Know-How and Troubleshooting Tips by Betty Barnden

Family Knits: 25 Handknits for All Seasons by Debbie Bliss

The Knitting Encyclopedia: A Comprehensive Guide for All Knitters by Claire Montgomerie

Loom Knitting for Babies & Toddlers: More Than 30 Easy No-Needle Designs by Isela Phelps

Natural Nursery Knits by Erika Knight

index

HILLSBORO PUBLIC LIBRARIES
Hillsboro, OR
Member of Washington County
COOPERATIVE LIBRARY SERVICES